"This book reminds us that we don't have to be to be superheroes to be brave; in fact, God should be the superhero in our lives! The five authors exhort us to become more Christ-like based on the teachings of James, and their honest testimonies and insightful commentaries really bring these familiar verses to life. Whether you are a new Christian or have been following Jesus for years, Only the Brave will give you a fresh take on discipleship, helping you enjoy the richness of living every single day for God."
 – **Debra Green OBE**, executive director, Redeeming Our Communities

"I'm excited that thousands of people will be engaging with this life-changing material. It's more than important that God's people wrestle with what the life of a disciple looks like and embark on the massive rollercoaster of being a world-changing follower of Jesus. Read on and get ready to be changed."
 – **Andy Hawthorne OBE**, founder and CEO, The Message Trust

"Seven times in Revelation 2–3, Jesus said: 'Anyone with ears must listen to the Spirit and understand what he is saying to the churches.' Only the Brave seems to have captured what the Holy Spirit is saying to the Church in our day. Its message is the timeless, biblical call to whole-life discipleship, but written for our times and context. It is easy to engage with, practical, and down to earth, and will help readers grow as followers of Christ."
 – **Steve Uppal**, senior leader, All Nations Church

"The vulnerability of the authors cannot fail to inspire a fresh look at our own journey with Jesus. The wisdom they bring from the book of James is challenging yet deeply encouraging for Christ followers who want to be ever more fruitful for Him in the adventure of everyday life."
 – **Tracy Cotterell**, managing director, The London Institute for Contemporary Christianity (LICC)

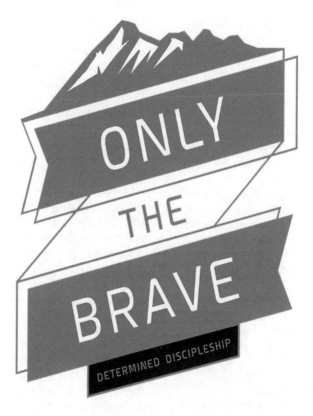

ONLY THE BRAVE

DETERMINED DISCIPLESHIP

A STUDY OF THE BOOK OF JAMES

LISA HOLMES
KRISH KANDIAH
SIM DENDY
CATHY MADAVAN
CRIS ROGERS

MONARCH
BOOKS

Published by Monarch Books
an imprint of
Lion Hudson Limited
Wilkinson House, Jordan Hill Business Park, Banbury Road, Oxford, OX2 8DR, England
Email: monarch@lionhudson.com
www.lionhudson.com/monarch

ISBN 978 0 85721 895 7
e-ISBN 978 0 85721 896 4

First edition 2018

Acknowledgments
Scripture quotations are taken from:
The Holy Bible, New International Version Anglicized. Copyright © 1979, 1984, 2011 Biblica, formerly International Bible Society. Used by permission of Hodder & Stoughton Ltd, an Hachette UK company. All rights reserved. "NIV" is a registered trademark of Biblica. UK trademark number 1448790.

The Holy Bible, New Living Translation, copyright © 1996, 2004, 2007 by Tyndale House Foundation. Used by permission of Tyndale House Publishers, Inc., Carol Stream, Illinois 60188. All rights reserved.

The Holy Bible, English Standard Version® (ESV®). Anglicized. Copyright © 2001 by Crossway, a publishing ministry of Good News Publishers. All rights reserved.

The New King James Version. Copyright © 1982 by Thomas Nelson, Inc. Used by permission. All rights reserved.

Quotations designated (NET) are from the NET Bible® Copyright ©1996-2006 by Biblical Studies Press, L.L.C. http://bible.org All rights reserved.

Extract p. 27 taken from "The Loneliness of Donald Trump", published on Lithub.com. Copyright © 2017 Rebecca Solnit. Used by permission of the author.

Extract p. 71 taken from *Christ the Controversialist* by John Stott, copyright © 1970 John Stott. Reproduced with permission of the Licensor through PLSclear.

Extract pp. 87–88 taken from "Loneliness in older people is a scandal. Here's what one church is doing about it" by Rev Steve Morris, copyright © 2017 Rev Steve Morris. Used by permission of the author.

Extract pp. 101–102 from "The transformative power of classical music", copyright © Benjamin Zander, TED2008 conference, 2008, TED.com.

A catalogue record for this book is available from the British Library

Printed and bound in the UK, February 2018, LH26

CONTENTS

ONLY THE BRAVE

JUSTIN WELBY, 2018

What do you think the most frequent command God gives in Scripture is? If we listen to debates and conversations in the church today, many answers come to mind: following, doing certain things, using the right words, praying, justice, personal morality, money, evangelism, going places, and so on. Well, actually, the most frequent command is, "Do not be afraid", which is a bit of a paradox because if anyone needs to tell us not to be afraid, it usually means there is something to be afraid of to start with!

Scripture is full of stories of God encouraging His people to take steps of faith, and saying, "Do not be afraid." It is also full of stories of God appearing to people and needing to say, "Do not be afraid." Simply standing before God, as we are, can be frightening and move us to respond as Isaiah did: "Woe is me, I am lost, for I am a man of unclean lips, and I live among a people of unclean lips; yet my eyes have seen the King, the Lord of hosts!" (Isaiah 6:5). Standing before God means having the courage to face who we are, and the consequences of who we are. It may not be fighting battles 'out there', but facing the demons within. Therefore we need to hear, "Do not be afraid."

But as we face ourselves, God also calls us to face how we relate to friends, family, other Christians, acquaintances, and the wider world. Facing ourselves and facing God is not an inward-looking, private adventure, but something that requires us to interact differently, and that may call us into unexpected places to do unexpected things. Courage is needed for the unknown; to follow wherever God may lead us, step by step, in our everyday lives. "Do not be afraid," God says.

It is all well and good to say, "Do not be afraid." But being told to be brave in itself is not going to help much! Fortunately, God never just says, "Do not be afraid." The command is always followed by something else. Most of the time, the something else is, "for I am with you". In other words: yes, there is plenty to be afraid of; yes, facing ourselves, facing God and facing the world honestly is a difficult task, which will require much of us, and may see us falter and fail at times.

But we are not alone. We do not have to drum up the courage from inside and find all the resources within us. The God we know in Jesus is going ahead of us, showing the way. He is going alongside us, holding our hand, and inspiring courage within us. He is going behind us, watching our back, ready to help us stand again after we fall.

In addition, it is more than God and me. God sends us out and leads us as part of His people. This is the very heart of the letter of James, which this book so powerfully explores. We face ourselves within the safety of God's love for us, in the company of others also called to face themselves. We are transformed by the work of the Spirit within us, together with others who can share the journey, in its highs and lows. We are called to live out our faith first and foremost in relationships: it is within the church, as James sees it, that we come face to face with the worst of ourselves; that we struggle with putting into practice the ideals we believe in. There is no romanticism in James about discipleship, about community, about church. It is hard, and we are required to trust God with the things we cherish, the things we fear and the things we hide. But in the face of it all, God said: "Do not fear, for I am with you."

Only the Brave starts with the presumption that we can be brave only because God is with us, and then indeed we are called to be brave. This has been the case for Christians throughout history, and it is still true today. The good news is that the bravery is not our screwed-together courage, but our response to the loving and empowering presence of God.

CALLED TO BE A DISCIPLE

CRIS ROGERS

I *woke up early in the morning,* packed my rucksack with food and water for the day, and headed out wearing my robust walking boots and cowboy hat. It was Easter weekend and I had been staying in East Jerusalem, following the footsteps of Jesus. Jumping on the bus out to the Judean desert, a small group of us headed into the wilderness to walk the 25 km road from Jerusalem to Jericho. It was hot, dusty, rocky, and hard work. The road was challenging, and I can certainly see why someone might be mugged on it. But it was worth it. To connect with a real place and a story Jesus told made me think afresh about what it means to live out the life Jesus called me to fulfil. Jesus called the early disciples to come and follow Him. The roads they followed were treacherous and often led to places other rabbis would never have gone. Following Jesus wasn't a stroll on a summer's day but demanding, difficult, dusty, and hot.

This book calls us to a life of following Jesus. Using the book of James as our road map, we are going to head out on a determined adventure through a rocky road of discipleship. We can't promise you that this book will not be challenging – any journey will have difficulty – but the life of a follower of Jesus is certainly an exciting one. We don't have to change to be loved by God, but if we are to love Him back, then there are going to be challenges we need to work through. Dorothy Day, an American journalist, social activist, and devout Christian, once asked, "Do you love the truth enough to live it?"

That is a great question. One that I have had to ask myself many times: "Do I love Jesus enough to live a life for him?"

It's too easy to simply believe in Jesus. According to James 2:19: "You believe that there is one God. Good! Even the demons believe that – and shudder." Even the devil believes in Jesus. What is going to be the stand-out, compelling, life-amazing action from your life that leaves the world aware not only of your belief but also of your passion for Jesus?

Only the brave are willing to not merely believe in Jesus but also to live it, love it, and share it. In a world that tells us to keep our heads down and try not to be noticed, my fear is that for many of us our greatest aspiration is to arrive safely at death. Mother Teresa reportedly said in an interview that rather than making it safely to heaven's doors we should hop, skip and jump through life. Don't play it safe; be playful in life. The life of a disciple is a disciplined life of following and copying Jesus.

It's this following and copying that makes the life of a disciple so unique. Our task is to get close to Jesus and follow where He is going. The ancient rabbis had young *talmidim* (what we would call "disciples") who would imitate their rabbi. They were students of the rabbi, watching intently, trying to catch moments that would help them live out the Scriptures better. They even used this phrase: "to be covered in the dust of your rabbi". The belief was that at the end of the day they had followed their teacher so closely they were covered in the dust he had kicked up on the road. But these young disciples weren't supposed to just *follow* the rabbi; they were also to *be like* the rabbi. They were to be copiers and studiers of their rabbi. For these young disciples it was a long road of watching and mimicking. There was no quick course but a life followed, watched, questioned, and imitated. You could say that being a disciple was like birdwatching. You sit for hours with nothing to see, and then spot a kingfisher jump out of the water. For a split second, the waiting is worth it.

Some of us behave as though discipleship is religious dabbling. This would never fit with the life of the disciples we see in the Scriptures. Then, discipleship meant catching the fire within Jesus, living this fire, and sharing this fire. They were passionate young men (and later young women) who burned with the desire to be like their Rabbi Jesus. Discipleship cannot be a half-hearted life but must be a life fully committed to Jesus' way in all areas of our lives: from our relationships, married life, dating and singleness, bank accounts, television habits, kitchen tables, shopping choices, political positions right through to our prayer life, Bible life, and worship life. Discipleship was always about the whole of our lives becoming wholly Jesus'.

Only the brave are willing to be *determined* to follow and copy Rabbi Jesus, to take the time to see His ways and allow them to permeate our ways. The title of this book, *Only the Brave*, does not mean it is for superheroes or superstars. *Only the Brave* addresses the gritty day-to-day life of a disciple that we all live. It's about the challenges we face, and about being a determined disciple in all the places our lives lead us. It's in the day-to-day that we all must find our courage to follow Christ. This is why it is so great to have five authors writing one book on discipleship. We each bring our own specialities, passions, and struggles. There is no one single kind of disciple; there is no cookie-cutter disciple. Here, you have five voices sharing on this journey in discipleship.

Discipleship in the Early Church

Together, we will explore the book of James alongside the patterns, challenges, and actions of a disciple. It is widely believed that the writer of the book of James was the brother of Jesus and the same

James found in the book of Acts who influenced the shaping of Christianity in Jerusalem. Having originally believed that Jesus was a religious extremist, he had avoided Him. Later, he became a believer when he saw the resurrected Jesus (1 Corinthians 15:7). James became a prominent leader of the church in Jerusalem and is mentioned in the book of Acts a number of times. He was involved in many of the debates regarding Christianity and the Gentiles, including the debate on circumcision. The letter of James was written in a very practical style, getting down to the basics of the faith and wrestling with the practicalities.

The early church saw massive growth. People needed to know how to live out what they were following. Often their old ways pulled them back, but James called them to take Jesus seriously and copy Him in all the areas of their lives.

Today, the book of James helps us explore the themes of discipleship practices and the life of a disciple. It challenges us to see how the predominant British culture is driving men and women to seek a life of pleasure and safety rather than the costly life of following Christ.

As with any letter found in the Bible, some knowledge of the circumstances into which the writer spoke helps us better understand the takeaway message. James was writing in a very unstable situation. The Jews were fighting to hold on to their identity. They wanted to remove the Roman occupation not only from Jerusalem but also from the wider region. The Romans were determined to restrain what they referred to as "these petty Jews" and maintain control. This tension left the political landscape shifting and fragmented. Meanwhile, most Christians were trying to keep their heads down. Some, however, chose to join the bloody revolts against the Romans and were martyred for their efforts. As a result, the Christian communities were scattered. James, writing to these Christians who were then in disseminated groups, called them to keep pushing through the persecution and cautioned them to be discreet to help stabilize things. James wanted the church to remain holy, to practise resurrection life, to be mindful of their words, and to have patience in the trials to come.

We will walk through the book of James chapter by chapter, drawing from the letter and asking what this means for us today.

WHOLE-LIFE DISCIPLESHIP

"Take up [your] cross and follow me," (Mark 8:34) is one of the first commands we read Jesus deliver. He wants us to go with Him and do what He is doing. Jesus is asking us to die to ourselves so that He might be born within us. This challenge is about seeing the whole of our lives impacted by Jesus. He wants our hearts and hands as well as our heads. Because we are people of *the Book* it is easy to make our faith book-based. We might base our faith on compassion and prayer, or we might be people who love to use our hands to serve. Perhaps some of us keep our faith locked up in a book, not wanting to engage with others or use what we have for God. It is possible to end up with big heads full of knowledge but small hands and hearts. And then there are those of us who might have large, compassionate hearts but little head knowledge and unformed hands.

Jesus was approached one day and asked what is the greatest commandment. He responded, "'Love the Lord your God with all your heart and with all your soul and with all your strength and with all your mind'; and, 'Love your neighbour as yourself'" (Luke 10:27).

Love God with your heart, your soul, your mind, and your strength. Taking this call to fully give ourselves to Christ, we understand that personal discipleship is about moving closer to what Jesus wants for us in all areas of our lives. We, the writers of this book, have broken this commandment down into three areas: our *head*, *heart*, and *hands*.

Head

Here we will be unpacking the book of James from a theological perspective. We will explore the challenge put to us and what we receive from it and grapple with it to make it a reality in our lives.

Engaging our minds in the text, we seek to find the balance between the lesson and how it applies to our daily lives.

Heart

Further exploring the theology, we reflect how James impacts and challenges our internal lives and how our hearts work this out in prayer, meditation, challenge, and rigorous realignment to Christ's ways. We challenge our dreams, expectations, and desires and align them with the heart of a disciple. This is about allowing our hearts to be changed, admonished, and redirected.

Hands

Drawing together the words of the text and the realigned heart, we ask how we now live this out with our bodies. How do we live like Christ in our actions? We get practical and real about the day-to-day life lived for Christ in our marriages, homes, workplaces, neighbourhoods, politics, healthcare, and so on. What action can we change because of what we learn about our heads and hearts?

Discipleship is about allowing Jesus to shape us in all areas of our lives: our heads, our hearts, our hands. James allows us to grapple with how we FACE the new reality through Jesus. We question how to LIVE out this new life. We hold the reality of things we need to TAME in becoming more Christlike. We determine what to LOSE to ensure sure we only carry what we need, and then we FINISH the faith race well.

So may our lives be shaped by Jesus as we:

> FACE IT
> LIVE IT
> TAME IT
> LOSE IT
> FINISH IT

MEET LISA HOLMES: interview by Cris Rogers

You're a Baptist minister in Skipton, North Yorkshire. What do you love about life in Skipton?

I was born in the South but always longed to live in the North, especially Yorkshire. Skipton is known as the Gateway to the Dales and I love the easy access to hills, dales, and sheep. Skipton is small enough to have a really great community feel and big enough to have great shops and cafes.

On a day off what can you be found doing?

Taking our dog Jess the whippet for a walk or run, drinking coffee, baking, playing the piano, or often just collapsed in front of the TV! Any of these might happen with Mike (my husband) or our two teenagers Caitlin and Joel.

Tell us a little about why discipleship is important to you personally.

I've known Jesus for many years but there's still so much to know about Him and learn about following Him. I love the challenge of never quite knowing where He's going to lead me next and it excites me that I can read a passage I've read many times before and God still speaks to me, challenges me, and changes me through that.

What do you see as the unique discipleship challenges in a market town?

Well, where I live has just been voted the happiest place to live in the UK. But you know, underneath the superficial loveliness there is still loneliness, anxiety, stress, mental health issues, marriage struggles, hunger, and debt. We are well programmed to hide these things – so perhaps the challenge is owning our need for Jesus and our dependence on Him, and making the sacrifices He calls us to.

What is it about the book of James that excites you personally for your own discipleship?

It's so down to earth – really gritty and practical. He talks about life and its challenges and pressures as they really are. I feel like he's challenging me to a life adventure that's worth getting up for!

FACE IT

LISA HOLMES

Do not merely listen to the word, and so deceive yourselves. Do what it says. Anyone who listens to the word but does not do what it says is like someone who looks at his face in a mirror and, after looking at himself, goes away and immediately forgets what he looks like. But whoever looks intently into the perfect law that gives freedom, and continues in it – not forgetting what they have heard, but doing it – they will be blessed in what they do.

James 1:22–25

There are some things that a person should never do by accident, and running two marathons in eight months is one of them. Last year I had a so-called "significant" birthday and I did quite a bit of thinking about what I'd achieved in my life and what I still hoped to do: the things that were "now or never".

In April, just before my birthday, like many people I was caught up in the excitement of watching the London Marathon on television – thousands of ordinary-looking people crossing the line on The Mall with so much elation and pride. I felt quite emotional and overly optimistic, and so, without due consideration for the possible consequences and without telling anyone, I secretly entered the ballot for the London Marathon. As I pressed "send", there was a strange mixture of panic and excitement with a big dose of reality. More than 253,000 people apply for the London Marathon and approximately 17,000 are allocated a place, so the odds were overwhelmingly stacked against me. I was going to be OK; there was very little chance of having to run anyway. However, over the next few months I had this unsettling but increasingly persistent sense that I *wanted* to run the marathon. Strange, really, as I would say that I'm a reluctant runner, and the most I'd ever run was a half marathon a few years before, and that was more than enough.

The feeling kept niggling away at me so I decided to enter the Chester Marathon with only eight weeks' training. I trained rigorously in that short time and on 2 October 2016 I lined up, feeling sick with nerves. Off I went, and only five hours and eighteen minutes later it was over. I DID it! I ran it. I had completed a marathon. Never mind the fact that I could scarcely walk. I never needed to run 26.2 miles again – and that's when it happened. Just one very short week later, a red, plastic-covered magazine dropped through my letter box with the words "You have a provisional place on the 2017 London Marathon" written in huge letters on the front. I didn't know whether to laugh or cry. Of all my friends, I had been given a place, and I was going to have to face a winter of long runs, cold mornings, rain, snow, determination, pain, Yorkshire hills, and mud, with the goal of successfully completing the most iconic marathon in the world. Oh, and winning a medal.

WHAT DO MARATHONS HAVE TO DO WITH DISCIPLESHIP AND THE BOOK OF JAMES?

I learned so much through that experience. Pushing through laziness and pain, being constant and not erratic in training, ignoring the weather conditions and doing it anyway, and taking responsibility for myself and not relying on others to do it for me, to name just a few. Many people have said that the journey of discipleship is a marathon, not a sprint. That seems a great picture to me. It's putting one foot in front of the other to follow Jesus. It is about consistent courage in the everyday experiences of our lives; it is, as the book of James reminds us, about determined discipleship.

There are many different themes in James' letter, but one thing that runs consistently throughout the narrative is the need for authenticity in our discipleship: true faith that has integrity; faith that is worked out in the way we live. There is never any sense that this will be easy – it will require bravery, determination, and persistence.

From the very beginning of his letter, James is completely open about the fact that following Jesus will be challenging, and that those trials are part of the way in which we are moulded and formed in our likeness to Jesus.

We should not forget when reading the New Testament that most of it was written to believers who were suffering and being persecuted, or at least marginalized, because they followed Jesus. Their lives were pressured on all sides, and it required bravery and persistence for them to be disciples of Christ.

Similarly, today, there will be external pressures that seek to destroy our faith. We may experience ridicule, discrimination, or even violence against us. There will be internal pressures too – temptations that seek to lead us away from God and His purposes. These may occur because of flaws in our character or because of particular inclinations we have or just because we are weary or discouraged by life's challenges. In the face of both external and internal pressures we are encouraged to stand firm and to persevere, to trust in God and look forward to the "crown of life" that will be ours (James 1:12). Just as I needed to train consistently for the marathon, so we need to practise our discipleship daily. Just as I needed to be disciplined in running and completing the race despite the desire at times to give up, so we are called to stand firm and persevere to the finish line.

RESPONDING TO GOD'S WORD

The section of James' letter that we are looking at focuses on our response to God's Word (James 1:19–25). It begins with a common metaphor, one that Jesus Himself used when He spoke about our response to God's Word. James speaks about the Word of God being "planted" like a seed within us, growing, and bearing fruit in our lives.

This has echoes of the parable of the sower in Mark 4 where the fruitfulness of the seed is directly in proportion to the quality of the soil. It is perhaps this thought that leads James to speak about the need to "get rid of all moral filth" in our hearts in preparation for us to receive God's Word. More than simply receiving it, believers are to *live* by the Word of God, allowing God's Word to speak to us, counsel and guide us, direct us, and shape us, as we orient our lives toward God. This part of James' letter is all about how we "respond" to God's Word, and James uses a couple of different images to enable us to understand what that means.

ONLY THE BRAVE

When our children were little, we watched a lot of films derived from fairy tales. One of their favourites was *Snow White*. In most of these there is one especially frightening, villainous character. In *Snow White* it is the wicked stepmother, who is known for her vile nature. You might recall that she had a magic mirror and every day she would ask, "Mirror, mirror on the wall – who's the fairest of them all?" and of course the mirror would say, "Oh, you are." He must have liked his job! But one day the mirror told her something different and she became extremely angry. Her reaction didn't make the fact that she was no longer the *fairest in the land* any less true, but in her anger she just wouldn't believe it. She became so angry that she was willing to murder Snow White because she was more beautiful.

Unfortunately, too many of us today are a bit like the stepmother in *Snow White*. We hold the Word of God, the Bible – what James referred to as a mirror – in front of us and often get angry or embarrassed because it is talking to us and about us and we don't like it very much. We don't want to be faced with the truth about ourselves. In discipleship terms, it is really "only the brave" who are willing to look in the mirror and see what is genuinely there and act on it.

James' thoughts on discipleship cluster around powerful images that capture our imagination and enable us to grasp more fully the concepts he wants to communicate. The crucial image here is the *mirror*, and the key verses of this short section are James 1:23–24:

> *Anyone who listens to the word but does not do what it says*
> *is like someone who looks at his face in a mirror and, after*
> *looking at himself, goes away and immediately forgets what he*
> *looks like.*

FACING UP TO REALITY

Many of us have had beach holiday experiences where we spend the whole day swimming and sunbathing and by the end of the day our hair is matted from salty water, wind, heat, and sand. Our faces are nicely made up with smears of sun cream and a smattering of sand and we are a mottled mixture of red, brown, and (at least in my case) freckles. We feel relaxed from a fun day out and feel great – until we look in the mirror and realize what a mess we must have looked coming home. On such occasions, we generally choose to *do* something about it.

The purpose of a mirror is to reflect reality so that we can – if we need to or choose to – change that reality. Of course, mirrors nowadays may be more about form and decoration, but we must remember their primary purpose is function.

We are surrounded by mirrors, or by reflective glass which acts as a mirror – too many and too much. In our homes, in restaurants, along the street, even on our phones, there we are again and again and AGAIN reflected at our best and worst. What we see in the mirror is a significant aspect of who we perceive ourselves to be. We make judgments about ourselves dependent on what we "see" in the mirror. Perhaps we find ourselves thinking, or even saying, "I really should lose some weight," "That doesn't suit me," "Is that some grey in my hair?" "Are there more wrinkles than there used to be?" "If only I had looked..." Perhaps it's not just in fairy tales that we ask the question, "Mirror, mirror on the wall – who's the fairest of them all?"

Mirrors have become such a powerful force for us all today, regardless of age, gender, or stage of life. My daughter is part of the "selfie generation": her image posted on Facebook, Instagram and Snapchat, out there for everyone to assess and judge, "like", or ignore. Phone filters are the way forward: we can enhance ourselves – make our eyes look bigger, make our nose look smaller, or even give ourselves cute puppy ears. Whatever we choose, we have the capacity to make ourselves look different and change people's perceptions of us – but it's not reality.

Our culture holds mirrors up to us so often that we use that reflection to define who we are. We are what we wear, where we shop, where we live, where we go on holiday. We are strongly influenced by our cultural mirrors. According to the website cityam.com, Fitness Knowledge reported that £250 million was spent on UNUSED health and fitness clothing in 2016.[1] At the same time, an average of around £550 per annum was spent on gym membership, with people attending an average of 13.5 times per year – meaning each visit cost around £40. We want to be fit; we want to look right while getting fit; we look in the mirror and attempt to conform to what our culture is telling us – but in reality we do not change. We are even influenced by what the media tells us are the best and worst places to live. Bristol and Dover won those titles respectively in 2017, according to the websites bbc.co.uk and ilivehere.co.uk.[2] Something of our identity is wrapped up even in our address. For all of those now feeling ecstatic or offended, you can just go to another website and there'll be a different result. Such labels remind me of the mirrors at a fairground where we recognize our image but it is distorted to a greater or lesser extent. We laugh, but we would be unhappy if that was what we truly looked like. And yet we far too easily trust what the media holds up in front of us with their similar levels of distortion. The sad reality is that all too often we don't even recognize this distortion. We are so accustomed to what we look like in the "cultural mirror" that we do not realize that the mirror presents us with a false or fake reality. The reflection has lied to us and made claims of us that simply are not true.

These are powerful visual realities, and it is almost impossible not to let our identity be impacted by what we see. It takes a brave person to choose to turn away from the mirrors that almost everyone else is using and to choose to assess their reflection, their image, their identity in a different mirror.

Equally, it takes a brave person to change the mirrors that they have been comfortably staring into because they reflect back what they want to see. The most extreme version of this is known as narcissism. This term originated from Greek mythology where the young man, Narcissus, fell in love with his own image reflected in a pool of water. Narcissism, according to the Oxford English Dictionary, is an "excessive interest in or admiration of oneself",[3] characterized by selfishness and self-centredness. It's a trait that is often seen in the most powerful. Simply expressed, "I am the centre of my world," and there is little, if any, openness to other views. The person is shielded from gazing into any mirrors other than those that communicate the truth as they see it.

Rebecca Solnit, writing on www.lithub.com in an article titled, "The Loneliness of Donald Trump", addresses something of this issue:

The child who became the most powerful man in the world, or at least occupied the real estate occupied by a series of those men, had run a family business and then starred in an unreality show based on the fiction that he was a stately emperor of enterprise… and each was a hall of mirrors made to flatter his sense of self, the self that was his one edifice he kept raising higher and higher and never abandoned.

I have often run across men (and rarely, but not never, women) who have become so powerful in their lives that there is no one to tell them when they are cruel, wrong, foolish, absurd, repugnant. In the end there is no one else in their world, because when you are not willing to hear how others feel, what others need, when you do not care, you are not willing to acknowledge others' existence. That's how it's lonely at the top. It is as if these petty tyrants live in a world without honest mirrors, without others, without gravity, and they are buffered from the consequences of their failures.[4]

CHOOSING THE BEST MIRROR

In all honestly, we all choose our mirrors, choose the standards we feel we already conform to, choose the people who will only tell us what we want to hear rather than those who will lovingly keep us accountable. Only those who are determined to become disciples of Jesus will have the courage to let the Word of God be their mirror over the mirrors of society that we can scarcely avoid, or the comfortable mirrors that might show a more favourable reflection.

A BRIEF HISTORY LESSON

The first mirrors were most likely pools of dark, still water or water collected in a primitive vessel. The requirements for making a good mirror are a surface with a very high degree of flatness (preferably but not necessarily with high reflectivity) and a surface roughness smaller than the wavelength of the light. The earliest manufactured mirrors were pieces of polished stone such as obsidian, a naturally occurring volcanic glass. Early examples in Turkey date back to around 6000 BC. Mirrors of polished copper were crafted in Mesopotamia from 4000 BC and in ancient Egypt from around 3000 BC. Polished stone mirrors from Central and South America date from around 2000 BC onward. In China, bronze mirrors were manufactured from around 2000 BC. Mirrors of speculum metal or any precious metal were hard to produce and were only owned by the wealthy. Stone mirrors often had lousy reflectivity compared to metals, yet metals scratch or tarnish easily, so they frequently needed polishing. Depending upon the colour, both often yielded reflections with inferior colour rendering. The poor image quality of ancient mirrors explains Paul's reference in 1 Corinthians 13 to seeing "as in a mirror, darkly". Glass was a desirable material for mirrors. Because the surface of glass is naturally smooth, it produces reflections with very little blur. Also, glass is very hard and scratch resistant. However, glass by itself has little reflectivity, so people began coating it with metals to increase the reflectivity. Metal-coated glass mirrors are said by the Roman scholar Pliny the Elder to have been invented in modern-day Lebanon in the first century AD, although no archaeological evidence of them date from before the third century. According to Pliny, the people of Sidon developed a technique for creating crude mirrors by coating blown glass with molten lead.

In ancient Rome, mirrors were a crucial element of society because cleanliness and grooming were highly valued in the Empire. Around AD 45, when James would have been writing this letter, mirrors were not widely available, and a good mirror was a precious commodity. To own such a prized possession, to have the opportunity to study oneself in it, and then to do nothing about the reflected image would simply be foolish, incomprehensible, and careless. The recipients of James' letter would have understood the ridiculous nature of what he was saying in a way that we might miss today with our abundance of mirrors.

James' challenge for us is to be a people who not only look in the mirror – the mirror that is Scripture – but also to be changed by it.

This mirror that Christ holds up to us is a reflection that not only changes us but also inspires us. Its purpose is to show us our failures and frailties, but also to enable us to see how Christ sees us and how we can be transformed. It neither flatters us nor *floors* us. While it almost certainly will require courage to look deeply into the mirror and bravery to respond to what we see, it is an experience entirely hopeful and grace-filled as we cooperate with the Lord Himself in being transformed as His disciples. He is the one who sees us as "fearfully and wonderfully made" (Psalm 139:14), who has lavished His love upon us (1 John 3:1). We are His masterpiece, His work of art (Ephesians 2:10). These are beautiful and affirming words. Perhaps if we spent much more time looking into that mirror we would value ourselves more highly and have a more Christlike perspective on who we are.

So, as disciples of Jesus, how can our thinking, our attitudes, and our actions be impactful?

For the past twenty-five years I have had the privilege of pastoring a local church. My calling day by day is to enable people to really understand what the Bible says as well as what it is saying to them personally. It's about walking with people as they work out what it means to be a disciple of Jesus and to become more like

Him. Sometimes I've done that really well and at other times I've made mistakes, but it is my joy to see people learning to love God with all their mind, soul, and strength (Mark 12:30) Our discipleship works itself out in this way, through head, heart, and hands.

HEAD: UNDERSTANDING GOD'S PERFECT LAW

As we focus on James 1:22–25, we see that James never shied away from being direct in his teaching. "Do not merely listen to the word, and so deceive yourselves. **Do** what it says" (James 1:22) [emphasis mine]. There is nowhere to hide in this verse; listening is not enough. We need to be alert to self-deception, to those times when we tell ourselves that we are engaging with God's Word when in fact we are only listening casually or selectively. James then uses the mirror comparison to reiterate and expand his point. The Word of God is like a mirror. Our response is to remember what the Word says, what it says to us and about us, and then act or live in the light of it. The revelation that God offers through His Word must be worked out in our lives as we follow Jesus.

In verse 25 the idea of self-examination is pursued further: "Whoever looks intently into the perfect law that gives freedom and continues in it – not forgetting what they have heard but doing it – they will be blessed in what they do." This verse takes James' readers back to the past and to a powerful history that resonates throughout the Scriptures, particularly the story of the Exodus, the moment of their liberation from Egypt and the giving of the Law. The Law enabled them to form their new identity as the people of God – a people loved by God, precious to Him, devoted to Him, holy to Him. It took just one night to take Israel out of Egypt, but more than forty years to get Egypt out of the people of Israel. After hundreds of years in slavery it wasn't easy for them to establish a renewed identity as God's chosen people. The Law helped them in that process of restoration. It is similar for us. We can commit our lives to Jesus as Lord but it may take years for us to be redefined, reformed, reshaped by God and His Word. That's our experience of discipleship.

Shaped by God's Word

A number of years ago, around February (I think it was a delayed New Year resolution), I decided it was time for me to recommit to a pattern of daily Bible reading rather than the somewhat haphazard approach that I seemed to have developed. Those of you who have or have had young children know that every waking moment is taken up, and by the time they are asleep and you've eaten, all you want to do is fall asleep yourself. That's where I was. Anyway, I decided to follow the Bible in a year plan that was suggested in *Word for Today*. In principle this was a great idea, but unfortunately, because I'd already missed January. I was launched straight in at Leviticus.

Amazingly, at least to me, God honoured my commitment to meet with Him as I read through this unlikely book. I suppose it is in the Bible for a reason but I had never stopped to think why. The verse that really jumped out at me and made sense of all the rest was Leviticus 9:6: "This is what the Lord has commanded you to do, so that the glory of the Lord may appear to you."

All these instructions, all these regulations, all these laws, all the things about what they could and could not eat or wear or do at certain times were shaping the identity of God's people. As they submitted to God in obedience they experienced more of the glory, the presence of God with them. *God communed with them, and it was a powerful motivation for holiness among His people.*

Something about this really hit home to me. God wants me to be holy so that His glory might be displayed – in me, through me. *God wants His people to be holy so that His glory might be displayed among them, in them, and through them.*

- **Does that excite and inspire you?**
- **Does that make you want to be holy?**

Holiness no longer fills us with dread at the thought of our lives going from technicolour to black and white. Instead they will be lives that are dazzling and radiant, vibrantly coloured with the glory of God.

Understanding God's Boundaries

There are rules; there are instructions; there are boundaries, but these allow us to be fully human. Living the way God instructs is the best way to live: *fully alive, fully connected to Him and to one another, and the inevitable consequence of that is that His glory shines out.* Boundaries are good because within them there is freedom and security. Remember, James writes that the person who looks intently into God's Law and acts on it experiences freedom (James 1:25).

Let me give you an example. A fish is made to swim in water. If a fish were to object: "I'm fed up with these rules. I want to travel, see a bit more of the world, experience things – how can I know my life is the best it can be unless I have something to compare it with?" And with a flip of his tail he's over the edge of the fishbowl. Whoa! For a minute, he can't get his bearings; everything seems a bit fuzzy. He doesn't feel quite right. It's not quite as thrilling as he thought. Then he spots... the cat. He flexes his tail to get away but nothing happens. He's not safe any longer – in fact, he's not free any longer – he's in mortal danger.

In the Law and within the whole of Scripture God gives us boundaries:

- **Not because He wants us to die but because He wants us to live.**
- **Not to restrict us but to give us security.**
- **Not to inhibit our freedom but to extend it.**

God gives us boundaries because He *loves* us. He wants the best for us, just as we seek to give our children boundaries because we love them and want the best for them.

The guidelines or boundaries of Leviticus could be split up into various areas: practical, spiritual, moral, and relational. We will look more at how that works out for us a little further on.

Jesus and the Law

When Jesus came and walked among us, He promised not to do away with the Law but to "fulfil" it (Matthew 5:17–18). Just before He said this, Jesus spoke the profound words we know as the Beatitudes, and He reminded His disciples that they were to be the salt of the earth and the light of the world. The rest of the Sermon on the Mount expressed what it meant for Jesus to be the fulfilment of the Law, what it meant to truly follow Him as His disciple, what it looked like to gaze in the mirror of God's Word and follow it.

The mirror Jesus used was like a high-definition version. The requirements of His disciples were costly. "You have heard that it was said... 'You shall not murder'... But I tell you that anyone who is angry with a brother or sister will be subject to judgment'" (Matthew 5:21–22). "You have heard that it was said, 'You shall not commit adultery.' But I tell you that anyone who looks at a woman lustfully has already committed adultery with her in his heart'" (Matthew 5:27–28). Jesus reached right to the heart of our motives, our intentions, and our attitudes.

Discipleship involves tough choices, long-term choices, choices that have integrity. Jesus compared the wide road that many travel on and the narrow path that few choose, but it is the narrow path that leads to life (Matthew 7:13–14). He spoke about recognizing the essence of a person in a non-superficial way – a bad tree will produce bad fruit but only a good tree will produce good fruit (Matthew 7:15–23). What is going on at the core of who we are? Where is our true life coming from? He concluded this profoundly significant section of teaching by focusing on the wise and foolish builders – the wise man who built his house on the rock and it withstood the storms, and the foolish man who built his house on the sand and it collapsed. Jesus introduced this final parable with these words that James echoes in his letter: "Therefore everyone who hears these words and puts them into practice is like a wise man..."

It is not simply hearing or reading the words, but taking action based upon them.

It is not simply glancing in the mirror and then forgetting what we see, but seeing ourselves as God sees us and behaving in the light of what we see.

For some of us, the honest truth is that our "mirror" is hidden away in the wardrobe or covered with dust under the bed, neglected, rarely picked up, and often ignored. What we need to do most is invest time in reading God's Word again. We aren't certain what God says about many things and we don't really know what He says about us. Sadly, the opposite can also be true. We know what the Bible says but we are embarrassed by it because it seems to conflict with the messages we are receiving from our friends, the media, and "what everyone thinks now". So we cover the mirror and choose to ignore it.

If we want to make living out the Bible a reality in our lives, here are some sample question to ask ourselves as we look at it.

- **Will I act on Jesus' words?**
- **Will I start to see myself as God sees me?**
- **Will I start to see others as God sees them?**
- **Will I start to behave differently in light of this?**

YES BUT HOW?

Find an accessible reading plan – something that works for you and will help you get to grips with God's Word again. Why don't you try E100 Journey through the Bible (http://e100.scriptureunion.org.uk) or what we called "E-Jesus" because we're from Yorkshire (http://e100.scriptureunion.org.uk/files/E100_planner.pdf)? We have used both of these in our church and been really encouraged by the many people who have taken up the plans and embraced the support and accountability of reading the Bible together with others.

Maybe you could choose one of the Bible in a Year books or plans? Many people have recommended Nicky Gumbel's *Bible in One Year* to me. If you're not keen on reading, you can listen to the Bible in your car or on your phone. You could even learn to sing the psalms and learn Scripture that way.

Perhaps you and some friends could read the Bible together or do the Wisdom Challenge. This entails reading one chapter of Proverbs each day for thirty-one days and sharing or posting the verse that most stands out to you from that chapter. Or why not choose one of the Gospels?

If these don't appeal to you, find something similar. There are many options out there. Don't be hard on yourself if you miss a day. Aim for two to three good sessions a week but try to get into a pattern. I find it really helps my concentration and understanding to write a few thoughts about the passage in a journal as I go along, and to try to reflect on what God is saying to me. A couple of my friends find that they like to draw a response to God or write out a particular verse artistically. Until we get to know God's Word we won't really be able to look into it and allow it to change us.

HEART: BEING WILLING TO "FACE YOURSELF" IN GOD'S MIRROR

Confession: I choose to believe some mirrors more than others. In my world, not all mirrors are equal. I have my favourite mirror, especially if I'm dressing for a special occasion or feeling a bit low on self-confidence. It's the mirror that I think makes me look just a little taller and a little slimmer – the one that, in all honesty, whatever the actual truth, makes me *feel* better about myself.

Let's face it, when we look in a mirror, often what we have is not so much a *cerebral* reaction as an *emotional* one. It's not our heads but our hearts that respond to the mirror's reality check or seeming criticism of what we look like. It's our hearts that glow warmly when who we like to think we are and our chosen mirror conform to one another. It's in our hearts that we bow to the cultural mirrors of consumerism or conformism. It's our hearts that hold the negativity or cynicism of the social network or media mirror.

Some of us are, or have been, surrounded by destructive people. People who say things to us that are hurtful, destructive, or dangerous. We all know people who by their words imply or make us feel that we are worthless when we are endlessly valuable, that we are stupid when we are smart, that we are failing even when we succeed. Others might only tell us what we want to hear, butter us up, are afraid to be honest with us perhaps because of the way we might react. In either instance, these people are not helping and they are not presenting our image in an honest way. They, and we, are limiting our true reflection. Whatever their intentions, they are not true.

Self-awareness is one of the most important interactions we can have with a mirror. Just as we see that an item of clothing no longer fits us so well or that our hair needs some attention, this personal attention is knowing what requires correction or action. Self-awareness can be defined in a number of ways but it is understood as gaining a clearer perception of our personality, including strengths and weaknesses, thoughts, beliefs, motivations, and emotions. It also allows us to better understand other people, and how they perceive us, our attitudes, and our responses to them. Self-awareness has a positively impact not only on us but on all our relationships.

Our reflection causes us to react in one of two ways. Either we tend toward pride: "I look great, better than _____," "I'm doing so well," "Yes, I can put a tick by that list of discipleship requirements;" or we tend toward a sense of worthlessness: "I look dreadful," "I'm so rubbish at this," "I'll never attain to that, ever." God's Word leads us to a *true* sense of who we are, how He sees us now, and how He longs to see us. We find that our true identity is in Christ. For this, what I call "transforming looking" (rather than glancing or even just looking), to occur we need to cultivate a spirit of humility.

In 2016, the Archbishop of Canterbury, Justin Welby, released the following statement:[5]

In the last month I have discovered that my biological father is not Gavin Welby but, in fact, the late Sir Anthony Montague Browne.

This comes as a complete surprise.

My mother (Jane Williams) and father (Gavin Welby) were both alcoholics. My mother has been in recovery since 1968, and has not touched alcohol for over 48 years. I am enormously proud of her.

My father (Gavin Welby) died as a result of the alcohol and smoking in 1977 when I was 21.

As a result of my parents' addictions my early life was messy, although I had the blessing and gift of a wonderful education, and was cared for deeply by my grandmother, my mother once she was in recovery, and my father (Gavin Welby) as far as he was able.

I have had a life of great blessing and wonderful support, especially from Caroline and our children, as well as a great many wonderful friends and family.

My own experience is typical of many people. To find that one's father is other than imagined is not unusual. To be the child of families with great difficulties in relationships, with substance abuse or other matters, is far too normal.

By the grace of God, found in Christian faith, through the NHS, through Alcoholics Anonymous and through her own very remarkable determination and effort, my mother has lived free of alcohol, has a very happy marriage, and has contributed greatly to society as a probation officer, member of the National Parole Board, Prison Visitor and with involvement in penal reform.

She has also played a wonderful part in my life and in the lives of my children and now grandchildren, as has my stepfather whose support and encouragement has been generous, unstinting and unfailing.

This revelation has, of course, been a surprise, but in my life and in our marriage Caroline and I have had far worse. I know that I find who I am in Jesus Christ, not in genetics, and my identity in him never changes.

Cultivating Humility

What exactly do we imply by the word "humility"? People often think humility is about being lowly, almost a doormat, but the Bible takes a different and much more positive approach. Godly humility starts when we see things as they really are – ourselves and other people – and realize that God is the maker of all things and the standard by which everything is measured or evaluated. This is not some kind of "comparisonitis" – a current affliction in our society where we constantly measure ourselves against others, whether they be a colleague at work, another family member, or an airbrushed celebrity. It is an appropriate, measured look at ourselves in the light of God's Word – His mirror.

We need to gaze into the mirror of His Word, willing to hear His correction about our attitude, our behaviour, our speaking, our love for Jesus. We must be willing to say in our hearts, "Yes, Lord," willing to submit to His authority and respond to what He says. We need humility to deny ourselves, our rights and opinions, our worldly comparisons, and say yes to Jesus' words. We need humility to make changes, to hold ourselves accountable and to realign ourselves with God's standard for discipleship.

We even need humility to agree with what God says about us when it's beautiful and affirming rather than believing our own "bad press", which is a form of inverted pride, because God's Word overcomes our own opinion. A key issue for us today is that we live as if the world revolves around us. We, at least in the West, have become known as the "entitled generation". Discipleship is the equivalent of a Copernican Revolution, where we understand that our world revolves around Christ. He is the centre. He is Lord. Humility is about submitting our "ego" – all that we are – to Him. Entitlement cannot coexist with humility. An attitude of humility before Christ and His Word allows us to be malleable, mouldable, and open to immense, life-transforming change in the Lord's hands.

- **Are we ready to be reshaped, re-created to be more like Jesus, our master?**

Mirror Issues

Sometimes we feel we look so bad that we want to avoid the mirror at all costs. (If you don't believe me, just think about the last time you had the flu.) This is also true in our discipleship. Spiritually, there are times when we just don't want to look in the mirror. We don't want to hear what God's Word says. Perhaps we hear the echoes of His voice inside our head and we are trying to drown it out, not amplify it. We make a conscious decision to choose to walk away from Jesus, not toward Him.

Instead of being responsive, our hearts become calloused, even calcified, and we epitomize those who look in the mirror, go away, and immediately forget what we look like (see James 1:24).

A major issue, particularly in Western society, is *body dysmorphia*. This is defined by the NHS as "an anxiety disorder that causes a person to have a distorted view of how they look and spend a lot of time worrying about their appearance".[6] We are sadly all too familiar with the distressing evidence of bulimia and anorexia among not only teenagers but also even people in their forties as we take our lead from the cultural mirrors that confront us daily and are unable to separate truth from fiction when it comes to ourselves. The sad reality is that people who weigh only a fraction of their optimum weight look in a mirror and see a person that they describe as "fat" or "ugly" or "grotesque".

It seems to me that there is also a case of spiritual or soul dysmorphia. We look at ourselves in the mirror of Scripture and what we see is not a true image; instead we exaggerate some flaw. We believe that we are judged and that grace can't extend to us; we are condemned and can never be forgiven, and we are considered failures who can never be restored or given another chance. Viewing ourselves in such a spiritually unhealthy manner destroys us rather than pointing us to Jesus. The evil one has shone a light only on certain parts of verses, certain aspects of Scripture, and neglected to show the whole. There is no perspective, and certainly not Christ's perspective, on His Word or indeed on us. Jesus spoke to His disciples about how it would be the Holy Spirit who would reveal the truth to them. He will convict rather than condemn and will remind us of all that Christ has said and our status as children of God (John 14:26; John 16:8–11; see also Romans 8:16). When we look in God's Word, the challenge is to truly hear and believe the words of affirmation and love that are written there. It is our opportunity to experience the grace of God and to have our confidence renewed in our identity in Christ.

MALCOLM'S STORY

God is so willing to restore us and help us to see ourselves differently. This is the experience of my friend Malcolm Duncan (also one of the Spring Harvest team). Malcolm writes:

I had a difficult upbringing and, as a consequence, I never felt very happy in my own skin. I was the kind of child who appeared confident, but the reality was that my external confidence was like a clown's costume. I wanted everyone to like me, I desperately wanted a place to belong and a sense of being loved, and I hid my insecurities and self-loathing behind the mask.

For as far back as I can remember, every morning when I woke up I would go into the bathroom, look in the mirror, and say out loud to myself, "You are stupid, you are ugly, and it is your fault." When anything went wrong, I assumed it was my fault. Because I was told that by others, I ended up, literally, telling myself that. Others self-harm by cutting their arms, starving their bodies, or doing something physical to themselves. I self-harmed by humiliating myself in the mirror every morning.

I was converted when I was sixteen but that daily mirror ritual did not change. I continued to seek other people's approval, I continued to be consumed by self-loathing, and I continued to believe that I was stupid and ugly and that it was my fault.

Then, when I was twenty-one, I had a powerful encounter with the Holy Spirit. God spoke profoundly to me at a concert in Motherwell one evening through the ministry of the Christian singer, Larry Norman, and I realized that God loved me unconditionally and that nothing would ever change that. I could never embarrass God and He would never reject me. I sobbed for three weeks from the moment I woke up until the moment I went to bed. My friends thought I was having a nervous breakdown but I knew what was happening. God was reaching into my broken heart and reshaping me. He was pulling out the heartbreak, the pain, the rejection, and the self-loathing.

After three weeks, my sobbing stopped. I remember the morning. It was a cold day outside and, when I woke up, I felt the sunlight on face; it felt like a gentle hand was soothing my cheek. There were no tears! I rushed into the bathroom of my small council flat and looked in the mirror and the voice in my head had gone. I looked at myself and for the first time in my life, I said, "You are loved, you are beautiful, you are gifted, and it is not your fault." The tears of sorrow and brokenness were gone and instead I fell on the floor in my tiny, shabby bathroom and wept for joy.

My morning ritual has changed. For more than twenty-five years I have been saying something different to myself every morning. When I look in the mirror, every day, I whisper, "I am loved. I am beautiful. I am gifted and it is not my fault." God is still reshaping me. When I hear the word "stupid", something inside me cringes. I know that every day of my life since that moment when I was twenty-one has been a day of walking into a deeper and deeper experience of a relationship with a Father who loves me deeply, accepts me completely, and will never leave me. The mirror – once the place where I reminded myself of how useless and rejected I was – has now become the place where I am reminded of how loved and accepted I am."

- Are we willing to really face ourselves in the mirror, even if it's difficult to look at what we see, and choose to listen to what Jesus says, whether that's His words of truth and affirmation that need to replace the half-truths or lies we believe, or whether it's uncomfortable stuff we need to address?

That's the challenge of discipleship, of closely following Jesus. He never said it would be easy or popular. In fact, He promised it would be costly and we would need to deny ourselves, even die to ourselves.

Cultivating Obedience

Blessing comes, as James 1:25 says, in obedience – in bravely choosing to face the mirror even when we know that we won't like what we see or when we feel that the Lord won't like what He sees in us. It means we take a really good, long look at ourselves and then have the guts and determination to cooperate with the transforming Holy Spirit to see the likeness of Jesus formed in us. The Holy Spirit often works in us as we read or listen to God's Word. He intervenes with us deeply to bring about a lasting change within us. He knows us perfectly and so, as we make ourselves vulnerable to Him, He brings about restoration in a way that is unique to us and our discipleship.

James 1:19 says that we need to be "quick to listen, slow to speak and slow to become angry". More often than not we are slow to listen, quick to speak, and fly off the handle at the first opportunity.

We need the exhortation to listen not just to one another but also to God.

Real listening isn't done with our ears alone but with our whole attitude and our bodies. Real listening requires effort, concentration, and a willingness to allow what the other person is saying to impact you at whatever level is appropriate.

Often this is not possible for us; we just can't listen properly. We are too busy, preoccupied with our own opinions. Maybe we are full of emotions that prohibit good listening. Our decks need clearing before we can incorporate James' metaphor. The flower bed needs clearing out before we can plant new seeds that will grow. James 1:21 exhorts us to "get rid of all moral filth and the evil that is so prevalent".

Cultivating the Soil of Our Souls

At the beginning of this chapter, we pondered Jesus' parable of the sower (Mark 4:1–20). This metaphor is about the preparation of the soil. It is key to the flourishing of the seed which is God's Word. In the same way as if we want to create a beautiful garden we need to do soil preparation, if we want God's Word to grow in us we need to invest some time in *soul preparation*. If we are truly committed to getting God's Word to take root and grow in our lives, we need to clear out those things that will prevent that happening, or make it more difficult. Soul preparation doesn't happen by accident, any more than soil preparation does. We need to decide and to be intentional around preparing ourselves to receive God's Word.

It may be behavioural patterns or habits that need changing, those which are simply unhelpful in enabling us to let God's Word grow in our lives – or even prevent it growing. Maybe we need to reassess how we allot our time in order to create space for God's Word to take root in our lives; perhaps there is unforgiveness and resentment that needs addressing so that we can hear God with a new freshness. Each one of us is different, and we all have contrasting experiences, but God knows exactly what we need to improve our reflection.

James says that we need to get our lives cleaned up so God's Word can get into us, and we need to acknowledge with humility that we need God's Word in us to change us and save us. *Our own self-sufficiency and independence is probably one of the biggest blocks to really listening and responding to God's Word.*

We must learn how to listen to God, to hear the promptings of the Holy Spirit. We have to recognize God's voice speaking in every circumstance of our lives, to expect that He will speak to us not only in church but also at work, in our homes, in the car. God always wants to communicate with us; we just need to learn to keep our spiritual ears open to Him. In my office I have a special chair, and my Bible, journal, pens, and devotional books are easily accessible to me. This space helps to create an environment where I am ready to listen to God. Other people find that God speaks to them as they walk and talk with Him in the natural environment. Good listening rarely happens rapidly, and making sure we make time to slow down in our frenetic lives is key to hearing God.

Reading God's Word with Our Eyes Wide Open

Just as there are times when we are actually keen to look in a mirror, so there are times when we are willing to look into God's Word and are receptive to what it says. In 2006 I became involved in the campaign Stop the Traffik, remembering the 200th anniversary of William Wilberforce's Act of Parliament to abolish the slave trade. My involvement took me to India to witness modern-day slavery and inspired me (along with others) to travel around the UK to explain the campaign and invite people to get involved. This work is still going on today. I can honestly say that it wasn't until I became involved in this that I realized how much the Bible has to say about justice and injustice. We all know the verses about the poor and marginalized, but it was as if the scales had been taken off my eyes and I could see everything differently. Sometimes our circumstances and experiences allow us to see the Bible with much greater clarity.

At other times we need to hear from God. When we are in need of comfort, hope, affirmation, or courage, we have a strong sense that God's Word will provide. We read it, hungry to be fed, eager to listen, with our eyes open to see what He might be saying to us. We pray for the Holy Spirit to enlighten us through God's Word. We come ready.

Even still, there are times when just reading a familiar passage in a different translation can really help to bring life to our interactions with Scripture. It helps us see familiar words from a new perspective and connect with our lives in a refreshing way. As disciples of Jesus, making sure we know the things He says and the way He says them is key to growing and to keeping going.

Listening Leads to Action

James goes even further in his challenge to us to listen to God's Word. His letter instructs us not to become complacent when we have listened to God's Word: *if you only listen, it's worthless; you need to do it.*

In 1912, during the maiden voyage of the *Titanic*, the on-duty radio operator received a message from another ship, warning of icebergs in the area. He put the message under a paperweight by his elbow and carried on with his work. It never reached the captain, and 1,500 lives were lost. *Information without action can result in destruction.*

That is a *big challenge* to us. Compared to doing, listening to God's Word is easy. It may make us feel uncomfortable or even guilty for a brief period of time, but once we've got away from the source of the Word we can usually find something to keep us busy, and the feeling fades. Doing, on the other hand, requires discipline: time, commitment, financial sacrifice, change.

Looking in the mirror takes only an instant. Our response to it, whether washing our face, shaving, ironing our shirt, or getting a haircut, takes significantly longer and requires more effort.

What is required of us is responsive obedience. This is a continued listening to and searching through God's Word followed by continual obedience and doing what we hear.

Some questions to think about:

- How are you developing the right attitude to reading and listening to God's Word?

- Is there an attitude or activity where God has been speaking to you and you are not listening?

- When you read and listen to God's Word, how ready and willing are you to be obedient to those things that the Holy Spirit highlights?

HANDS: RESPONDING TO WHAT WE SEE IN THE "MIRROR"

When our HEAD and HEART are on track, how do our HANDS react?

If we return to the LAW, we see a very practical outworking of God's Word.

Practical Holiness

God is practical because holiness is so practical.

Our house is a bit damp. We live in Yorkshire and it rains a lot. Mildew is a frustrating problem for us, especially in our back porch. A while ago I took off the peg a coat that was hanging at the back and it was covered in mildew – yuk. We took all the coats down and more than half of them were mildewed. Some were so bad we threw them out. It's lethal; it spreads and it's difficult to get rid of even with the strongest detergents. That's why God told the Israelites to throw away mildewed clothes (Leviticus 13:47–59). He told them to burn anything with mildew to protect everything else. He is very practical. He cares about everything, even our wardrobe.

Here is another example from Leviticus: God was concerned about the Israelites' health so He advised them against eating animals that were high risk and advised them on matters of hygiene (Leviticus 5:2–3; see also Leviticus 11–15).

In the same way that God is concerned with the details, holiness is not some airy-fairy state we get into when we have been to a spiritual conference. Holiness affects *every aspect* of our daily lives. *It's about how we spend and invest our money, how we treat our colleagues in our workplaces, the kinds of things we put into our bodies. The Hebrews had a holistic approach to spirituality – everything mattered to God.*

So what about fair trade? Environmental issues? GM foods? Junk food? Smoking? Drugs? Employment legislation? Political affiliation?

There's an apocryphal story about a group of church leaders who were robustly condemning the fact that the speaker they had just been listening to seemed to have supported a funding application to the National Lottery. These leaders were enraged. The more they talked about it, the more upset they became, until the tears started to flow – down their cigars and into their whisky glasses. Well, of course, it's just an amusing story, but it makes the point that what for one Christian is a "non-negotiable" in terms of holy living is not the same for another, and we find it easy to judge one another's choices in these matters.

Jesus told a parable about removing the plank of wood from our own eye before we try to take the speck out of someone else's. This is supposed to make us laugh – at ourselves and our ability to see when someone else is wrong, missing something, not being obedient to God's Word, without recognizing our own blind spots and addressing those first.

What would God say about these things that I've mentioned? How should practical holiness affect your day-to-day life? How could God's glory shine more brightly through the way you live?

- **Through your finances?**
- **Your shopping choices?**
- **Your travel to work or school?**

- Your housework?

- Your time management?

God is concerned with practical holiness through lifestyle choices that honour Him. His Word should make a difference in our homes, our workplaces, our leisure activities, our lifestyle choices. His Word is worked out in the normal stuff of our lives.

- Look at your bank statement for the last month. Where did you spend most of your money? This is an indication of what is important to you.

- Have a look at your diary for the past six months. How do you invest your time? What does this say about your priorities and where your discipleship most needs to be worked out? Where can you make changes that reflect God's Word?

Spiritual Holiness

This primarily covers areas associated with sacrifice and worship. God is concerned with those who will worship him in "Spirit and in truth" (John 4:24). He is looking for those who will bring him a "sacrifice of praise" (Hebrews 13:15). We no longer require the right location, the right robes, the right animals – Jesus has given us direct access to the Father in heaven. Now our critical need is for the right attitudes and holiness of life. We come to worship with clean hands and pure hearts.

How does the way you worship express your response to God's Word? I find that God's Word is often the best springboard for my worship. From the Psalms I fill my mind with truths about who God is and the wonderful ways He works, and I find my heart echoes the psalmist's in a desire to seek God and draw near to Him. Reading and responding to Scripture enables me to engage with the Lord in a much deeper way; it also challenges any complacency I might have.

In Matthew 5:23–25 Jesus reminds us that we are offering our gift at the altar. If, while we are there, we remember that someone has something against us, then we should leave our gift and go and be reconciled to that person first. I wonder how often I have ignored this. I wonder how many worship times are impacted by the unresolved relationships represented in the room. I also wonder how many relationships and churches would be transformed if we were to live in obedience to this command. To be honest, there have been a number of times over the years when I have phoned home and apologized before leading a service or searched someone out to resolve an issue before I could wholeheartedly worship. This is what spiritual holiness looks like worked out in our lives.

How does your daily relationship with the Lord demonstrate your open access to Him? Are you cultivating a greater intimacy with Him that makes it clear that He is the centre of your life? Does His centrality in your adoration displace any other "idols" that threaten to rise up and take centre stage? Idols are simply those things that replace Jesus in our lives; anything that we are more committed to than Jesus himself; anything that comes first when we have chosen to call Him "Lord". We only need to take a look at what we devote our time and money to in order to see where the possible idols are in our hearts. The challenge is to love Jesus more than all these other things and put Him at the centre.

Moral and Relational Holiness

God is concerned with moral and relational holiness. At the heart of God is relationship based on self-sacrificial love.

God created human beings to be in relationship with Him and, from that relationship of love and security, to be in relationship with others. Genesis 1:26 says, "Let us [implying Father, Son, and Holy Spirit] make mankind in our image, in our likeness." From the very beginning we derive our identity and purpose from God Himself and we are created to function in community, in relationship with others, like the Godhead. God wants our relationships with others to reflect the relationship He intended to have with us, but, of course, sin has entered the equation and spoiled what God has given for good. Satan's aim, in the name of freedom, is to break down all the boundaries God has given for our protection to make everything possible and permissible. In these books, beginning with the books of the Law but encompassing all of the Bible, is God's intent to guide His people for their well-being. God invented relationships; he created sexuality and intimacy, and He knows what leads to wholeness and happiness and what does not.

How we behave in our relationships is probably the clearest evidence of how much time we spend looking in the mirror of God's Word and addressing the things we see in our lives as a result.

There are quite a few chapters in Leviticus that none of us would probably be too keen to read out loud – they're kind of embarrassing because of the issues they address. This made me think about the sort of embarrassing topics God would have to address with us today. These are the areas where God's Word gets worked out. One of those issues would, I'm sure, be pornography. Elaine Storkey writes in her book, *The Search for Intimacy*, "The saddest thing is that pornography can never be a substitute for relating to another human being. It can only widen the loneliness."[7]

Pornography is incredibly damaging to current relationships if we are married and to potential ones if we are not, and in truth will affect us and our relationship with God and other people whatever our "status". That person we lust over will never walk off the screen. Real people get hurt by addictions to fantasy ones. Real people can never live up to airbrushed images. Real people have issues and make demands. Real people know that we are not perfect either.

The struggle with pornography is now on the church's agenda. This has become a crucial issue as pornography is paralysing people within the church, and the church is largely failing to offer hope and constructive help to those beyond its doors to combat the issue. David Partington calls pornography "one of the most powerful weapons the enemy has ever used".[8]

Within my own church we have had the courage to bravely face pornography. It has not been easy, but we have had the guts to look in the mirror and not be afraid of addressing this area of people's lives. By providing a safe place, we have enabled people to be honest and vulnerable with us. We have walked with them and supported them as they break free of habits and destructive behaviour that has often dogged them for years. We have prayed for them and encouraged them to meditate on God's Word often as they see Jesus' transforming grace at work in their lives. We have struggled, but it has encouraged us that change is possible.

The truth is that if you have *any* ongoing struggle with addictive behaviour, change requires persistence, determination, and the right kind of support. That's what discipleship is all about – encountering Jesus as we are and then allowing Him to transform us one day at a time.

If you struggle with any significant issue, it is possible for you to change, but it may be difficult. The first step is honest and brave admission. It may be that you need a "mirror moment" – a catalyst moment where you see yourself in the light of God's Word and you decide that with the power of the Holy Spirit and the support of accountable friends you will change.

One of the most powerful films I have ever watched is *The Shawshank Redemption*. In the book by Stephen King, Red (played by Morgan Freeman in the film) describes how it feels to be incarcerated for almost forty years: "At first you can't stand those four walls, then you get so you can abide them, then you get so you accept them... and then, as your body and your mind and your spirit adjust... you get to love them."[9]

The commentator William Barclay wrote in his Commentary of John's Gospel, "The first step toward receiving the power of Jesus is wanting it! If in our inmost hearts we are content to stay the way we are, there can be no change."[10]

That's the real question: do you want to change? It's the same question that Jesus asked the two blind men sitting by the roadside: "What do you want me to do for you?" (Matthew 20:32). Perhaps it seemed obvious that the man would want to be healed, but Jesus gave him the opportunity to say yes or no to that degree of change. What we have always been or done easily becomes our identity, and change can be a bit scary, even if it's good change. Are you prepared to leave the security of the prison walls?

Often, all we need is a bit of determination, the courage to face the issue. It can be immensely helpful to have an accountability friend, someone to check in with, someone you give permission to ask the tough questions and with whom you choose to be honest and vulnerable. At other times we need more help and support. Many have found the Twelve-step Programme to be life-changing, for example. CAP (Christians Against Poverty) supports Release Groups through local churches to enable people to break free and live differently.

Maybe for you it's a completely different issue – a moral issue, a character flaw, some kind of behavioural pattern or lifestyle choice. The question is the same: do you want to change? Are you willing to take another look in the mirror and do something about what you see?

If your answer is yes or even maybe, then there is hope. In fact, there is a lot of hope for you.

OVERCOMING FEAR

Last year as a family we went to the Big Church Day Out in the North. We had recently acquired a campervan, one with a pop-up roof. We arrived in the evening, got ourselves organized and then got ready for bed – kids on the bottom, adults in the top. I wriggled into my sleeping bag, exhausted and looking forward to sleep. But instead of drowsiness streaming into my body, there was adrenalin. It began to course round my veins and in a moment it was as if I was propelled out of my sleeping bag, down the space into the bottom of the van and out of the door, my heart pumping and my body shaking. Claustrophobia, the fear of confined spaces, was the culprit. Eventually, after I had calmed down, I climbed back up, turned my face toward the outside and, after a horrible night, fell asleep briefly with the dawn.

I had lived with this phobia my whole life but had managed to deal with mostly by avoidance, but now it was beginning to limit my enjoyment of life and the activities I wanted to enjoy with my family. It was time to face it. There are no quick fixes to phobias – the way to change is by going through them. So I signed myself up for some help – a course of CBT (Cognitive Behavioural Therapy). I decided that it was time to face my fear and work through it.

What limits your life is probably different, but the question is the same: are you willing to face it?

In the closing part of this section, we consider James 1:25, which says, "But whoever looks intently into the perfect law that gives freedom and continues in it – not forgetting what they have heard but doing it – they will be blessed in what they do." We know from the rest of James' letter that this doesn't mean that we will always be happy or that life will always be easy for us. James tells us that we will face trials (1:2), and some of the most faithful and obedient disciples face unrelenting suffering, so what does this mean? James is exhorting his readers to take hold of the truth that contentment, the life that we were created to live, even joy, is to found in whole-life obedience to God and His Word. Both our challenge and our strong motivation is that by continuing to look into the mirror and responding to what we see, we will become more like Jesus, disciples who are like and act like our Master.

Before you leave this chapter:

- **Sit in front of a mirror for five minutes without interruption. Set a timer. Find three things you like about yourself.**

- **What are your strengths and passions? What are you good at? What do you like doing?**

- **What ONE thing does Jesus want you to face up to now in your discipleship? How are you going to do that?**

Further Reading

David Watson, *Discipleship* (Hodder, 2014)

Oswald Chambers, *My Utmost for His Highest* (Discovery House, 2012)

Ajith Fernando, *The Call to Joy and Pain* (Crossway, 2007)

Michael Frost, *Exiles: Living Missionally in a Post-Christian Culture* (Baker Books, 2006)

John Ortberg, *The Life You've Always Wanted* (revised edition, Zondervan, 2002)

Gregory A. Boyd, *Present Perfect: Finding God in the Now* (Zondervan, 2010)

Sam Allberry, *James: for You* (The Good Book Company, 2016)

Alec Motyer, *The Message of James*, Bible Speaks Today (IVP, 1985)

Testimony from Fiona, 44, Glasgow

I'd never considered myself brave until I was diagnosed with an aggressive form of breast cancer earlier this year. As I went through four months of chemotherapy, surgery, and then radiotherapy I found that time and time again people told me how "brave" they thought I was. I have to admit it puzzled and slightly frustrated me as I did not feel at all brave! In fact, I often found myself feeling very scared and alone, and I saw my treatment as something that I simply had to endure if I wanted any chance at life, not something that I was "brave" to face. I have changed my mind slightly as I look back on this year, though – bravery, like courage, isn't necessarily about not being afraid; it's about carrying on in a challenging situation anyway. For me, it became about how to trust God for a future that felt very uncertain.

Without a doubt my breast cancer diagnosis has been the biggest challenge I have faced so far in my life. Becoming ill is one of those possibilities that lurks in the mind of every healthy person, but it doesn't prepare you for the shock of being diagnosed and entering months of treatment.

I am very fortunate to have a wonderful support system of family and friends. In the initial hours after finding out I had cancer, I had this crazy plan to keep it a secret, to not tell anyone except perhaps one or two people who would have to know. I now realize how difficult I would have found that, and how much love and support I would have missed out on – the practical things people did, the emotional support, and the prayer support have all been part of my treatment.

I don't know how people face this kind of life-changing event without Jesus. I don't mean that in patronizing way; I simply mean that were it not for my faith I'm really not sure how I would have coped, as it was so hard even with a strong faith! I do remember realizing it was a real kairos *moment for my faith: here was where the rubber would hit the road. Did I actually believe all I had paid lip service to for all these years of being a Christian? Could I really believe all would be well, even if my body would not recover from this disease? I've had some hard moments in it all but I do know I haven't been alone – I've immersed myself in the Psalms, and particularly in verses of lament. I wanted to finish this year knowing Jesus better than I did at the start, and all it's made me want to do is keep knowing and loving Him better.*

I'm so thankful for everyone around me this year: our wonderful NHS, all my family and friends. I had read quite a bit about how gratitude can change your perspective, and in the dark, early days of my diagnosis one of the things I used to do to try to keep calm and refocus my mind was to make a list of ten things I could give thanks for that day. They could be ridiculously small things, like a good cup of coffee, but it really did help me to thank God for my life that day and thank Him for His goodness.

MEET KRISH KANDIAH: interview by Lisa Holmes

Krish, we know family is massively important to you. Please tell us a little about your family.

I am married to Miriam and together we have three birth children and three adopted children. It's a busy house, especially as we also do emergency foster care for babies, but I love the sense of fun and togetherness it brings. Our youngest two children have additional needs and I count it a great honour to learn to see the world through their eyes. Recently I bought a couple of fridge magnets for them from an overseas trip and they literally jumped for joy. I am learning from them how to experience joy in the ordinary.

You are the founding director of the charity Home for Good. What motivated you to begin the charity and what inspires you about it most?

The more I read Scripture, the more I realize that God is particularly concerned about the most vulnerable people in our communities – that must include children who are not able to live at home with their parents. And the more I fostered children, the more I understood of God's love and grace in adopting us into His family. If my worship of God and my pursuit of justice did not influence how I did family and work, then I would have very little credibility to my profession of faith.

On those occasions when you get to have time off, what is it that you find most enjoyable and relaxing?

I love meeting new people and exploring new places. I love that I often get to do that through and with my family and work. I also enjoy books and reading and being part of a book group. We have met together every month for the last ten years, and we challenge each other to think and reflect on books about economics, science, philosophy, history, and politics.

What is it about the book of James that you get excited about?

I love James' no-nonsense approach. I love how he calls us to radical and brave discipleship. I love how he challenges us to care for the poor and to stop seeking to please the rich.

Where do you think we need to be particularly brave as disciples?

I think we need to be brave about being known as Christians. Brothers and sisters around the world are dying for their love of Christ or making great sacrifices in their commitment to Him. I think we can all learn from them to be willing to be publicly associated with Christ and obey Him whatever the cost.

LIVE IT

KRISH KANDIAH

What good is it, my brothers and sisters, if someone claims to have faith but has no deeds? ...faith by itself, if it is not accompanied by action, is dead.

James 2:14, 17

I *am grateful for the friends in my life* who love me enough to ask me tough questions about how my life and faith are going. When I was at university I had a couple of mates I would meet with regularly to read the Bible, pray, and talk about some of the challenges we were facing. We didn't have a name for it then, but today some would call it an accountability group or peer mentoring. Three young guys living away from home, trying to work out how to be Christians in a new and challenging environment, we had a lot of fun together, but there was also some straight talking and dealing with big issues in our lives. I am eternally grateful for the influence these friends had on me, and I can't even imagine where I would be today without God working through these young men in my life.

As I read the book of James I have that same feeling of gratitude as I did with my mates at university. James is such a straight-talking book. As we saw in the last chapter, it's a mirror that helps us see ourselves in the light of God's perfect Law. Reading the epistle can be uncomfortable. But as we read it, the epistle of James is like a faithful friend daring to ask us the tough questions about our life in God. No matter how challenging the words appear to us, we know God, the one who inspired these words, is the most loving being in the universe. I can't promise you it will be an easy ride, but be encouraged, as the Proverbs tell us, "Wounds from a friend can be trusted" (Proverbs 27:6).

In this chapter, we are going to explore what it means to live out our faith. In the previous chapter, we have been urged to face up to the truth that God's Word exposes in our lives. We were challenged not only to read the Word, but also to do what it says. So now we will explore what James had in mind when he called us to live it out. Strangely, the heartbeat of James' challenge was not what most people assume to be the essence of Christian discipleship. I can't recall ever seeing James' definition of Christian worship in any discipleship book or course, so be prepared for God to ask some difficult questions of us. Before we can be ready for the practical challenge of James, we need to first address a challenging theological question the epistle throws at us. So it's time to get our heads engaged.

HEAD: ARE WE SAVED BY FAITH OR WORKS?

As a child I used to have great debates in the school playground about imaginary battles between legendary super heroes: could Batman beat Spiderman in a fight? How about Superman versus the Hulk? If I ask these questions to my teenage boys, they roll their eyes. "Wrong universe, Dad." What I can never remember – but they always do – is that Batman belongs to the world of DC Comics while Spiderman is from the Marvel universe. It has to do not just with copyright but also storylines. It means that never the twain shall meet on the big screen – which I find a little disappointing.

Who would win in a debate between New Testament epistle writers Paul and James? Is this the ultimate biblical superhero battle? Are we to expect a great showdown when we get to heaven? The great reformer Martin Luther thought Paul would win hands down when he wrote about the writer of the epistle of James:

> *I consider that it is not the writing of any apostle. My reasons are as follows. First: Flatly against St. Paul and all the rest of Scripture, it ascribes righteousness to works.*[11]

So, there you have it. Luther, one of the key figures in the Reformation, read a conflict here and backed Paul, calling James' letter just an "epistle of straw".[12] In fact, he even attempted to have the book removed from the canon of scripture so that it would not be one of the sixty-six books that the church recognized as being inspired by God. James 2 is the passage at the centre of this controversy. We need to first apply our minds to look more closely at this controversy, and then discover what James has to say about the way we live and love God.

Is there a Battle Between Paul and James?

The supposed conflict between Paul and James revolved around how we are actually saved. Whereas Paul teaches that salvation is a gift of grace received by faith and not by works, James appears to teach that salvation does rely on works, as though we have to earn our way to God:

> *What good is it, my brothers and sisters, if someone claims to have faith but has no deeds? Can such faith save them? Suppose a brother or a sister is without clothes and daily food. If one of you says to them, "Go in peace; keep warm and well fed," but does nothing about their physical needs, what good is it? In the same way, faith by itself, if it is not accompanied by action, is dead.*
>
> *But someone will say, "You have faith; I have deeds."*
>
> *Show me your faith without deeds, and I will show you my faith by my deeds. You believe that there is one God. Good! Even the demons believe that – and shudder."*
>
> **James 2:14–19**

Was James directly challenging Paul's understanding of the gospel? Did this undermine all of Paul's teaching? For us, does this indicate that the Bible is not trustworthy? Both in our personal lives and in the life of the church there is a temptation to be selective in our approach to Scripture. Many of us have what we could describe as a "working canon". By this I mean key passages that shape our understanding of the rest of the Bible. There are scriptures that have become very dear to us: the verses we underline, the parables we quote most often, the psalms we hang on our walls, the letters that are most often preached in our churches and conferences. At one level this is entirely understandable: the Bible is a library of sixty-six books and it can be hard work to master all of it. There are scriptures that seem particularly resonant for a phase in our lives or a time in history. Then there are verses and passages that the Holy Spirit specifically impresses on us.

When the great social reformer William Wilberforce suffered a nervous breakdown after persistent failed attempts to end the transatlantic slave trade, the great hymn writer John Newton quoted the Bible story of Daniel in the lions' den to him. He explained the similarities between Daniel and Wilberforce: both, he said, were men of public influence who found themselves in great difficulty.[13] One particular verse from the book of Daniel became an important motivating force in Wilberforce's life. Referring to Daniel 6:20, Newton said to him, "the God whom you serve continually is able to preserve and deliver you, he will see you through."

Many Christians talk about having a life verse, or a favourite passage of the Bible. For me, much of my ministry in the last ten years has stemmed from a verse God laid on my heart when we first began fostering children – James 1:27:

> *Religion that God our Father accepts as pure and faultless is this: to look after orphans and widows in their distress and to keep oneself from being polluted by the world.*

The challenge of this verse has opened my eyes to themes throughout Scripture about God's heart for the vulnerable.

We can see how Luther, in the middle of his epic Reformation fight against ecclesiastical institutions that insisted God's favour was earned or bought with penances and indulgences, would particularly love Paul's teaching on grace and faith. It is understandable that certain passages might have been "eureka" passages that changed the course of his life, and thus he went on to have a massive impact on church history, passages such as Ephesians chapter 2:8–9: "For it is by grace you have been saved, through faith – and this is not from yourselves, it is the gift of God – not by works, so that no one can boast," or, "the righteous will live by faith" (Romans 1:17; other examples might be Galatians 3:11; Hebrews 10:38).

Do We Really Trust the Whole Bible?

Favourite passages and eureka verses that change our *lives* is one thing. But when they change the way we *read the Bible*, we need to be careful. We can end up being selective and only reading the parts that match our passions or agree with our views. When we do this, either consciously or subconsciously, we turn the Bible into an ideological text. Scripture becomes a mascot for our views rather than a means for God to speak to us. We requisition God's Word for our own purposes rather than allow the living Word to speak to us and transform us. We become the master; God's Word becomes the servant. Taken to an extreme, this approach over the centuries has meant that the Bible has been used to justify some terrible things, from the Ku Klux Klan's white supremacist racism, to the justification of terrorist bombing of civilians, to domestic violence. If we find these things offensive – and we should – then we must be extra careful to ensure we allow the whole of Scripture to speak to us, without censoring it or editing it or ignoring whole swathes of it.

It is not for nothing that Paul explained, "All Scripture is God-breathed and is useful for teaching, rebuking, correcting and training in righteousness" (2 Timothy 3:16). Or that Jesus said:

> *"Do not think that I have come to abolish the Law or the Prophets; I have not come to abolish them but to fulfil them. For truly I tell you, until heaven and earth disappear, not the smallest letter, not the least stroke of a pen, will by any means disappear from the Law until everything is accomplished."*
>
> **Matthew 5:17–18**

Within the different streams of the church I have often noticed that we fail to take this whole-Bible approach seriously. We can see this evidenced in our teaching programmes, what we choose to focus on in our sermons, or the way the Bible functions in our worship – if at all. Despite the wonderful things that Luther helped the church to recapture, we cannot follow his example of filtering out the parts of the Bible that appear to challenge or disagree with what we think is important. We can't dismiss James as "an epistle of straw". We must let all of Scripture address us. With that in mind, we must figure out how we can hear both Paul and James when it comes to the role of faith and works in our salvation.

So How are We Saved – is it Faith or Works?

Before we take a look at how to reconcile Paul and James, there is one more important person we need to bring into the conversation: Jesus. To demonstrate that we cannot take sides between Paul and James on the role of good works in our salvation, we should perhaps read again Jesus' parable of the sheep and the goats (Matthew 25:31–46).

The scene is set at the end of time itself, with Jesus as the glorious King installed on His rightful throne and all the nations gathered before Him. He calls everyone individually, placing them either on His left or on His right. This action divides the characters into two groups and shows us what Jesus requires of us in order for us to make the cut.

Jesus first identifies those who are blessed by His Father, who have an inheritance and kingdom waiting for them. This is no ordinary extension of hospitality. Here the Lord of heaven is welcoming His people into a place that has been prepared for them since the creation of the whole world. Who gets to be in this group gathered together from all the nations? Those who have shown hospitality to Jesus. How have they shown hospitality to Jesus? In the way they have welcomed the stranger. Those who have not welcomed Jesus in as the stranger are excluded. Worse, they are sent away to eternal punishment.

Those who feel they need to edit out the epistle to James for fear that it teaches salvation by works would have to do the same with Jesus' teaching here too. And those who would edit out Paul are also in difficulty. The night He died, Jesus welcomed the thief on the cross as His plus one guest into Paradise (Luke 23:32–43), even though the man had no time or opportunity to do a single good work. So, if we cannot edit Scripture, how can we reconcile these different voices?

Perhaps we need to see the themes in Paul, James, and Jesus as different lines of music in a choral score. Perhaps it is possible to harmonize their different perspectives into a more beautiful and glorious whole, where each voice adds to the wonder and splendour of the performance. In the same way, Paul, James, and Jesus are not in conflict but rather contribute to our whole understanding. That's why God has included them in His revealed Word, the Bible.

There are three important melodic lines that we need to hear.

First, We are Saved by Grace Through Faith

Paul is very clear in Ephesians 2 that we are saved freely and only by the grace of God: "For it is by grace you have been saved, through faith – and this is not from yourselves, it is the gift of God – not by works, so that no one can boast" (Ephesians 2:8–9). This passage and similar verses led the reformers to crystallize what we now consider essential to the Christian faith: we are saved *Sola Gratia* (by grace alone), *Sola Fide* (by faith alone), and we know about this *Sola Scriptura* (by Scripture alone). This approach makes sense of so much of the big story of the Bible. If there was a way that we could have made ourselves acceptable to God, there really was no need for Jesus to be crucified. If there was any other means by which we could be saved, then why, when Jesus cried out to his Father in the Garden of Gethsemane, would God refuse to take the cup of suffering away (Luke 22:42) from His agonizing Son? None of us can point to our own merit, ability, or wisdom in becoming a Christian; we can only point to the freely given grace and mercy of God, and accept it in faith.

Second, Our Faith is Demonstrated Not Just by What We Say, but by What We Do

James does not contradict Paul's articulation of how we are saved. Indeed, James' explanation of how we actually become Christians sounds a lot like Paul: "He chose to give us birth through the word of truth, that we might be a kind of firstfruits of all he created" (James 1:18). In Romans 10:17, Paul wrote, "Consequently, faith comes from hearing the message, and the message is heard through the word about Christ." And in 1 Corinthians he speaks about the resurrection of Jesus being "the firstfruits of those who have fallen asleep" (1 Corinthians 15:20). But James goes on to explore the relationship between the confession of our faith and the demonstration of our faith. When James asks hypothetically, "if someone claims to have faith but has no deeds? Can such faith save them?" (James 2:14), he clearly expects the answer to be no. He is not questioning whether or not we are saved by faith. Instead he is asking: how can we know if we have genuine faith?

James insists that we show our faith ultimately through our lives, not through our words. This is not dissimilar to Paul's teaching in the verse immediately following the oft-quoted proof-text for salvation by faith (cited above). Ephesians 2:10 says, "For we are God's handiwork, created in Christ Jesus to do good works, which God prepared in advance for us to do." Paul couldn't have been clearer. We are not saved by our good works – salvation is a free gift of grace from God. But having received that grace, we are transformed, and one clear evidence of this is doing the good works that God has given us to do. In other words, we are not saved *by* good works, but we are saved *for* good works. Once we are connected by faith with Jesus (Paul calls this being "in Christ"), then our lives are changed to be *like Christ*. Christians are those who are "like Christ" (the name "Christian" literally means "little Christ"; Acts 11:26). This is evident in the parable of the sheep and the goats too. Jesus is the one who feeds the hungry, clothes the naked, and welcomes the stranger. But if we are connected with Christ through faith, this sort of living will become our normal, almost unthinking behaviour. Nicky Gumbel, vicar of Holy Trinity Brompton, said, "You are never more like God than when you are helping hurting people, lifting up the fallen and restoring the broken."[14]

Third, it is Our Response to the Vulnerable that is Particularly Important

Matthew 25 and James 1 both help us understand what "good works" means by showing us that caring for the vulnerable is the litmus test of our profession of faith. We shall explore this in the following section in more depth. But for now it is worth noting how many of the biblical authors pick up this theme, for example:

John:

> *This is how we know what love is: Jesus Christ laid down his life for us. And we ought to lay down our lives for our brothers and sisters. If anyone has material possessions and sees a brother or sister in need but has no pity on them, how can the love of God be in that person? Dear children, let us not love with words or speech but with actions and in truth.*
>
> **1 John 3:16–18**

Proverbs:

> *Whoever is kind to the poor lends to the Lord, and he will reward them for what they have done.*
>
> **Proverbs 19:17**

> *Whoever oppresses the poor shows contempt for their Maker, but whoever is kind to the needy honours God*
>
> **Proverbs 14:31**

The righteous care about justice for the poor, but the wicked have no such concern.

Proverbs 29:7

Paul:

All they asked was that we should continue to remember the poor, the very thing I had been eager to do all along.

Galatians 2:10

We can see these ideas lived in out in the book of Ruth, the prophecy of Amos, and the laws of Deuteronomy.

James, Jesus, and Paul – and indeed the rest of the God-inspired biblical authors – all seem to be on the same page when it comes to showing that our faith is demonstrated through the way we treat vulnerable people. However, assuming that because we serve the poor we have earned the right to eternal life is just as foolish as assuming that the increasing number of candles on our birthday cake is making us older or that standing on the bathroom scales is making us heavier. There may well be a correlation between positive pregnancy tests and pregnancy, but babies do not come from blue lines, just as obesity does not come from bathroom scales, and maturity does not come from owning multipacks of candles. The link is not causal but indicative. The same is true for good works and saving faith. There is a link, but the first does not cause the second. Rather, saving faith is indicated by good works. Just as we know a true prophet by their fruit and a wise builder by the longevity of their buildings, so we can know a true believer, says Jesus, by their response to the needy.

HEART: WHAT IF I DON'T FEEL LIKE I AM SAVED?

In a number of countries I have visited, I have been attracted to market stalls selling knock-off products available on the grey market: Ray Benn sunglasses, Joke-a-Cola and Abbibas trainers, for example. These products had a charm about them as they didn't take themselves too seriously, and for the frugal shopper they offered a pretty cheap alternative to the authentic branded goods. But sometimes the labels claimed the items were genuine. They may have looked indistinguishable to the products they were emulating, but a sip or a touch and you knew you had bought less than you bargained for. There is a frightening line of argument in Jesus' teachings where He explains that no matter what we have called ourselves, whatever label we may use to describe our faith affiliation, many of us will find out too late that our salvation was never a done deal.

Throughout his epistle, James raised the question as to what authentic faith looks like. We have seen that although we are saved through faith alone, the test of whether we have faith is not just our profession of faith. James calls us to see care for the vulnerable as an expression of our faith, and he comes up with what at first sight is an unlikely indicator: "to look after orphans and widows in their distress" (James 1:27). Often, before I am allowed to speak at an event, I am asked to sign a doctrinal statement, which is basically a test to see if I hold to orthodox Christian faith. Interestingly, I have never been asked whether I practise what I preach, or, more specifically, whether I care for vulnerable children or vulnerable adults.

At baptisms, we normally ask candidates (or their godparents) to confess their allegiance to Jesus, their belief in the Trinity, and their commitment to the church. In a counselling session, if someone is doubting whether they are really a Christian, we don't normally quiz them on their ministry involvement with the sick, the homeless, or the elderly. In interviews for full-time Christian work, a candidate is unlikely to be asked how they practically demonstrate mercy to those who are most in need. No. It has become standard practice for us to test the authenticity of someone's profession of faith on the intellectual contents of their beliefs rather than in the practical outworking of those beliefs.

But the epistle of James is very clear what the test for authentic faith is: "Religion that God our Father accepts as pure and faultless is this: to look after orphans and widows in their distress and to keep oneself from being polluted by the world" (James 1:27) . For James, evidence of someone's orthodoxy (right confession) is his or her orthopraxy (right practice). He looks beyond the profession of faith to a practice of faith. Commitment to God is shown in commitment, not just to our family and church, but also to strangers – and the most vulnerable ones at that. Jesus taught the same when He told the parable of the Good Samaritan in response to the question how to fulfil the two greatest commandments – to love God and to love your neighbour.

Just in case the words of Jesus and James are not sufficient to convince you that caring for the needy is intrinsic to our worship of God, Isaiah spells it out very clearly as he conveys God's distaste for the worship practices of His people:

> *Yet on the day of your fasting, you do as you please*
> *and exploit all your workers.*
> *Your fasting ends in quarrelling and strife,*
> *and in striking each other with wicked fists.*
> *You cannot fast as you do today*
> *and expect your voice to be heard on high…*
> *Is not this the kind of fasting I have chosen:*
> *to loose the chains of injustice*
> *and untie the cords of the yoke,*
> *to set the oppressed free*
> *and break every yoke?*
> *Is it not to share your food with the hungry*
> *and to provide the poor wanderer with shelter –*
> *when you see the naked, to clothe them,*
> *and not to turn away from your own flesh and blood?*
>
> **Isaiah 58:3–4, 6–7**

It's hard to think of a more widely recognized sacrificial spiritual discipline than fasting – enduring a level of physical pain by going without the nourishment and sustenance of food. But God says their fasting is a waste of time because it is just an outward religious ritual disconnected from the actual care for the needy. What James, Jesus, and Isaiah teach us is that, no matter how hard we try, we cannot replace our responsibility to demonstrate the compassion and grace of God with ritualistic religion. No matter how loud we sing, how much we pray, how many church services we attend, or even how much of the Bible we read, we miss the entire point of our faith if we do not serve the needy. The kind of worship that God is looking for is not satisfied by the rituals of our religion; it must involve compassionate service.

FAITH AND WORKS

The different streams of Christianity have often struggled to make sense of the challenge of passages like the parable of the sheep and goats, the relationship between faith and works, or the teaching of James 1:27 in different ways. By exploring three ways in which they have been misunderstood, we may be better able to avoid the pitfalls in our own understanding.

First, some streams of the Christian church have lived as if Christian worship and discipleship revolve around the knowledge and understanding of Holy Scripture. This stream takes some of the emphasis in Paul's theology on doctrine and somehow neglects Paul's other teachings and the wider teaching of Scripture on the importance of obedience. The epistle of James helpfully warns us of the dangers of confusing the knowledge of Scripture with obedience to Scripture. John Stott puts it eloquently when he writes:

To suppose that salvation lies in a book is as foolish as supposing that health lies in a prescription. When we are ill and the doctor prescribes some medicine for us, does he intend that we should go home with the prescription, read it, study it

and learn it by heart? Or that we should frame it and hang it
on our bedroom wall? Or that we should tear it into fragments
and eat the pieces three times a day after meals? The absurdity
of these possibilities is obvious. The prescription itself will not
cure us. The whole purpose of a prescription is to get us to
go to the chemist, obtain the medicine prescribed and drink
it. Now the Bible contains the divine prescription for sin-sick
souls. It is the only medicine which can save us from perishing.
In brief, it tells us of Jesus Christ who dies for us and rose
again. But we do not worship the Bible as if it could save us;
we go to Christ. For the overwhelming purpose of the Bible is
to send us to Christ and to persuade us to drink the water of
life which he offers.[15]

A second stream of the church that has misunderstood this balance in Scripture is one of socially active Christians who have given the impression that it is through our participation in bringing social and political change that we are saved. Sometimes this has been implied; other times it has been directly argued. The logic of this approach to the gospel is that humanity was going astray and so Jesus came and gave us a moral example of how to live better lives. It is through emulating the life of Jesus that we can save ourselves and our world. As with most forms of heresy, there is a grain of truth in this understanding of the Christian message. Yes, Jesus was morally perfect, and so emulating Christ is the way that God wants us to live. But if that was all that was necessary, there was no need for Jesus to die on the cross. The crucifixion of Jesus was not just a moral example; it was Jesus laying down His life for us so that by believing in Him we can escape the punishment that our sins deserve. Commitment to serving the needy, welcoming widows and orphans, is not a means by which we can earn our forgiveness from God but is rather a response to the grace of God that has already been shown to us. We should beware of preachers who give their congregations only practical ways to respond to the Bible. Churches that measure their success by the number of people on the hospitality rota or the food bank committee or the children's programme are likely to be missing an important aspect of the gospel.

The third way that some streams of Christianity misunderstand the challenge of passages of Scripture like James 1:27 and Matthew 25 is to replace actual physical effort toward meeting the needs of the vulnerable for an emotional or spiritual alternative. In other words, they seek to care for the souls of the widows and children. Or they focus on feeding those who are spiritually hungry, those who are emotionally vulnerable. This can, like the first category, focus on the expounding of the Bible to meet those needs. Or it can focus on providing a sentimentalized worship experience. We can know that these are at play in our churches when the effectiveness of a sermon comes to be measured by how many people made an immediate response at the end of it, or how many people are "touched" by the worship. When these quantitative measures are paramount, the temptation is that our services can revolve around the emotional response that needs to be elicited at its conclusion. Although spiritual and emotional responses to the gospel are not bad in themselves, focusing solely on this aspect impoverishes the congregation. It often does not lead to long-term change or to releasing people to draw close to God outside of the Sunday services.

When we consider our heart response to God, we often think of our sung worship, the emotions we express to God. But James offers us another way to think about our emotional life in connection with God. Rather than focusing on how passionate we feel about God, we should consider whether our passions and concerns for the world match God's. If we are not showing the same concern that God has for the vulnerable, poor, needy, and marginalized, then, James, Isaiah, and Jesus tell us, we are not really worshipping God. Whatever our emotional state, however caught up in wonder we are, to whatever degree we think we sense God's presence, the strong warnings of James 1:27, Matthew 25, and Isaiah 58 suggest that we may be deluding ourselves and depriving ourselves of true, intimate relationship with God.

How Can We Be Sure of Our Salvation?

So what should we do if we are feeling nervous about the state of our salvation? What if these challenging scriptures make us doubt whether we are truly part of God's family? The first response is, "Good." This might sound harsh, but these passages are deliberately trying to make us ask this very question. The Bible implies that there are many people in the world who have a false assurance of salvation. There are those who think they are in the kingdom because they have prayed a prayer at an evangelistic event, because they once felt something of God in their lives, because they attend church regularly, because they know their Bible well, because they believe in God, or because they have witnessed God's miraculous intervention in their life. But none of this is critical. Even the demons believe in God, says James (James 2:19). Even driving out demons, says Jesus, does not guarantee a relationship with Him (Matthew 7:23). These challenges are supposed to unsettle us. We are to be vigilant about false assurance because so much is at stake.

On the other hand, Jesus graciously offers us hope and a firm foundation in life. The role of the Holy Spirit in our lives is to act as a guarantee of our right standing with God. As Paul explains, it is He who gives us confidence to call God, "*Abba*, Father" (Galatians 4:6). Being in a permanent state of panic about our salvation does not help our discipleship or serve God's mission in the world.

A good articulation of this balance between accepting God's grace in our lives and wondering if we are really saved is expressed in a letter that John Newton, author of the hymn "Amazing Grace", wrote to someone wrestling with this very issue:

1.   *I am not what I ought to be...*
2.   *I am not what I might be...*
3.   *Not what I wish to be...*

4.   *I am not what I hope to be...*

5.   *Not what I once was....*[16]

This balance is so helpful. Newton explains that when he measures himself against the witness of Scripture and the person of Jesus, he falls far short. But he also recognizes that he no longer wants to live in sin. He wants to live a life of holiness, of service to God and neighbour, and this is a far cry from where he used to be. It might not be a linear growth curve of ever-increasing holiness, but there has been a tangible difference in Newton's life. Newton also recognizes that God is transforming him, and one day, by God's grace, he will be holy and wholly like Christ.

Sometimes I try to measure my ministry and I find myself frustrated. Have I wasted my time on projects that have not borne fruit? Have I made any headway at all into the huge needs of the world? Have I missed vital opportunities that God has given me? I love Newton's sense of peace and assurance. If I am no longer indifferent or inactive when it comes to caring with and for the most needy people in our world, then something has changed in me. I am not what I once used to be – selfish and uncompassionate. And this is only because of the grace of God acting in my life.

HANDS: HOW DO I LIVE OUT A LIFE OF GRACE AND FAITH?

As I walked home from McDonald's, my head was spinning and my heart was pounding. It wasn't just the sugar or caffeine rush from the Coke or the fat overdose from the Big Mac. It was because my brain was being rewired and my heart expanded through a challenging conversation with a friend. At the time I was a Chemistry student, but all my effort was going into leading the university Christian Union, which mostly involved running events. After one particular event I treated the speaker to a McDonald's meal, but talking about the church's role in justice and peacemaking was a discussion that took much longer than eating the fast food we had ordered. As we talked late into the night, my young understanding of the gospel was challenged by someone willing to take the time to help me think through the grand sweep of the Bible. The visiting speaker had helped a lot of people come to faith in Jesus earlier in the evening, and that night he opened my eyes to parts of Scripture that I had manage to ignore. Passages like these:

> *Learn to do right; seek justice.*
> *Defend the oppressed.*
> *Take up the cause of the fatherless;*
> *plead the case of the widow.*
>
> Isaiah 1:17

> *Do not take advantage of the widow or the fatherless. If you do and they cry out to me, I will certainly hear their cry. My anger will be aroused …*
>
> Exodus 22:22–24

> *Religion that God our Father accepts as pure and faultless is this: to look after orphans and widows in their distress and to keep oneself from being polluted by the world.*
>
> James 1:27

That visiting speaker became a mentor to me, and later the best man at my wedding. These passages led him to find some urgent practical Christian responses to the HIV crisis affecting the poor, widowed, and orphaned people of Africa, at a critical time before vaccinations and disease management were involved. What would it mean for me, as a Chemistry student in my final year of university? I wanted to serve God, of that I had no doubt. But I had a passion for preaching and evangelism. Wouldn't I be spreading myself too thinly if I were to try to do everything? Was God really asking me to be involved in social action as well, caring for those in poverty, or for vulnerable children and adults?

It was a challenge that has forever stuck with me. I went on to work for student ministry organizations and found myself assigned to an evangelism and discipleship project in the poorest country in Europe. Each day we came across orphans lying in the streets, begging, and widows dressed in black and barely surviving. It seemed very reminiscent of the patriarchal society of the ancient world where widows were particularly vulnerable, and it was often difficult for women to earn a living to support themselves. These widows were dependent on public charity and were often vulnerable to exploitation and abuse. The children lying in the street, we discovered, were the property of those who would use them and their begging to earn a living. The younger the child, the more pennies would be collected. And nobody seemed to be able to stop it.

The Bible presents those of us who call ourselves Christians with the responsibility of fighting for and caring for the needs of the marginalized and the vulnerable. It often mentions orphans, widows, and strangers as three groups of people that are especially in need of care and compassion (Exodus 22:21–22; Deuteronomy 14:29; 16:11, 14; 24:17; see also Jeremiah 7:6) . These categories of children and adults, made vulnerable because of family breakdown, death, or displacement, remain as relevant today as they were then. We are still called to look out for the homeless, the destitute, refugees, the elderly, people with disabilities, those who are trafficked or persecuted, or victims of natural disasters. The list could go on.

Orphan Care

When my wife and I returned to England to continue our ministry, we could not just leave behind the plight of the street children we had seen. The very least we could do, we decided, was to help one child in care in the UK experience a loving home. Our journey to adopting that one child has taken many unexpected turns, and now we have three birth children plus three adopted children as well as a growing number of children who have been part of our family through fostering. As we have seen so far in this chapter, it is clear that we are all called to care for the vulnerable as we have opportunity. I want to look at what it means practically for us to obey James' call to care for orphans in the UK and beyond.

In Hebrew, the word "orphan" referred to any child who had lost their father, irrespective of whether the child's mother was living or not. In a male-dominated society where fathers were the chief providers and protectors, "to be fatherless meant vulnerability to poverty and disenfranchisement".[17] The term "vulnerable child" is therefore equivalent in meaning to the Hebrew term "orphan", which in English has come to indicate only a child who has been bereaved of both parents.

In the UK at the moment there is a crisis in the care system, which is bursting at the seams and which requires our urgent attention. For a start, there are more than 50,000 vulnerable children on child protection registers. These are the children whom social workers have identified as at continuing risk of physical, emotional, or sexual abuse or neglect. But this may be the tip of the iceberg. The National Society for the Prevention of Cruelty to Children (NSPCC) comments:

> *Child protection plans are not a measure of the incidence of maltreatment but do give some indication of the scale of the problem by providing figures for the number of children who are judged to be at risk of significant harm. However, research indicates that abuse and neglect are both under-reported and under-recorded.*[18]

There are some very practical things that we can do to care for vulnerable children in the UK care system that allow us to demonstrate our faith through our works and offer God the "true religion" that He asks of us. Here are some examples.

Foster

Many people assume that foster care is something you do if you are short on money, qualifications, or job opportunities, but may have a spare room. However, Christians who understand that the call of God is to practise true religion and reflect His grace have a different vision. Foster care is an opportunity to help children who have been removed from their families under tragic circumstances. Foster care is an opportunity to welcome children in need into a loving and caring family environment so that they can be safe, they can be loved, and they can flourish.

I have met many amazing foster carers who provide so much more than a bed and breakfast arrangement. They go above and beyond the call of duty to provide a loving home and a healthy environment where the children can truly belong. I have met foster carers who have had to fight for children with disabilities to be treated fairly in their school. I have met carers who have given up family holidays so that foster children don't have to be left behind. I have met carers who have turned their home into an assessment centre for child refugees so that they wouldn't have to be "processed" in a hostile environment. These carers understand the call of God to care for the vulnerable, and the majority of them tell me that even though it is hard, it is a privilege. Through caring for these children, they have felt closer to God than they ever thought possible.

Adopt

Many people assume that adoption is something that you do if you are short on children or fertility or sense. Adoption is a fantastic way to form a family – not just for the infertile, but for anyone. However, currently, the majority of people who come forward for adoption are unable to conceive or carry a baby to term. And often for these adopters, the children waiting for a match are not the kind of children they are looking for. This is why in the UK there are lots of adopters waiting for children but also lots of children waiting for adopters – most adopters are prepared to wait for the young, healthy baby they imagine. Children who are slightly older, from toddlers to teens, do not tend to fulfil adopters' criteria. They often come in sibling groups, they may have additional needs, and many have experienced neglect or abuse. Many adopters feel that they are not willing or able to look after children in these circumstances.

However, there is a growing number of people who are coming forward to adopt a child who would otherwise never have a family to call their own. For Christians who understand that they have been given clear instruction to show our love for God by caring for orphans in their distress, there is a very different motivating factor. Children in care are not a means to an end – to bring joy to parents who cannot biologically produce offspring of their own. Children in care are valuable in their own right, and it is an honour to welcome the least of these into our families.

This kind of altruistic adoption is not to be entered into lightly. This is a labour of love that can be very challenging. Children who have had a difficult start in life do not change overnight. The abuse and neglect and feelings of shame and helplessness can last for years, if not a lifetime.

As I travel the country, I have been challenged and moved as I have met Christians who have chosen to pour love into children whom others would ignore or overlook: children with Down's syndrome; children who come in sibling groups in multiples of two, three, even four; children who have already experienced multiple placement breakdowns. These are children with names and surnames, with hopes and dreams, with gifts and talents, with families and futures. Each one matters to God and matters to their new and forever family.

Support

Not everyone is called to foster or adopt children. But as a church we need to live up to our calling to be a welcoming community. I have been to many churches that have embraced a vision for fostering and adoption and have radically changed their churches to make sure looked-after children are made to feel welcome.

I think of churches that say at the end of their services, "Mums, dads, and carers please go and collect your children from Sunday school." Just the inclusion of the word "carer" signals to the church that fostering is normal and that children from all sorts of backgrounds are welcome. I think of churches that have redesigned their children's and youth programme to make sure that children with additional needs are made to feel included. I think of "foster aunties and uncles" who have wrapped around foster families and their children to make sure they receive the support they need from the wider church community. I think of churches that have encouraged people to consider a vocation in social work, in family law, in art or play therapy. I think of churches that have set a prayer target to see more foster carers and adoptive parents in their church family. I think of Christian teachers that have been able to understand the needs of their pupils better because they have experience of seeing their church welcoming and supporting children in care. I think of house groups that have adopted a foster family, providing babysitting, ironing, food deliveries, and respite care to families who are looking after children who have had the hardest start in life. I think of churches that provide a safe space in their building during the week for fostering families, birth families, and social services to use.

Perhaps your church is in an area where refugees are beginning to settle. Maybe you are next door to a children's home, a halfway house, a nursing home, a school, a job centre, a drop-in centre. Perhaps your home is a place where some of the vulnerable people represented by these services can find a bit of love and Christian compassion. There are so many, many ways we can be involved in hands-on caring for the vulnerable.

The epistle of James makes a very direct call for us to "look after orphans and widows in their distress", and the challenge of Jesus in the parable of the sheep and the goats seems to be direct and personal hospitality: "I was hungry and you gave me something to eat, I was thirsty and you gave me something to drink, I was a stranger and you invited me in" (Matthew 25:35). In both of these passages, this direct intervention is both encouraging and challenging. Jesus offers us very practical things to do to serve Him. You don't need to be wealthy or powerful in order to serve Jesus. If you have even a cup of water and a morsel of food you can serve Christ by sharing that with someone in need. But it is also very challenging because often we try to minimize the impact that needy people will have on our lives by substituting direct engagement for sending money or joining a campaign. A monthly standing order supporting an agency that is working with the vulnerable can sometimes be a costly and wise sacrifice, but it can also be a cop-out so we don't actually have to get our hands dirty. As well as the direct contact with vulnerable children, there are, however, important ways that individuals can engage in caring for "orphans" as James instructs us. Let's explore three areas.

School

According to a recent report from the Children's Commissioner Anne Longfield, there are about 580,000 children, roughly the same number as the population of Manchester, who are so vulnerable that social services have had to step in and provide care or support in the past year. The same report showed about 800,000 children aged five to seventeen suffering from mental health disorders, and in the region of 200,000 children who were judged by their local authority to have experienced trauma or abuse. In England alone there are 1,200 newly identified victims of modern child slavery each year. This means that statistically there are going to be vulnerable children in your local school.[19]

Child protection and safeguarding are often seen as the boring part of school life, yet schools are often the first place where abuse or neglect is spotted. Many schools are struggling with diminishing budgets, and most are in need of governors and Parent Teacher Association members. If you are a parent or carer, might God be calling you to use your influence in the school to speak up and look out for the needs of vulnerable children? Often within the social network of the children at school there are children who are marginalized socially. If you are a parent or carer, what can you do to help your children be inclusive in their friendships? What can you do to reach out to other parents who don't quite fit in?

Politics

There have been huge cuts to the budgets of local authorities. As a foster parent, I have seen first-hand the difference this has made to the caseloads that social workers have to carry and to the outcomes for children. I believe we need more Christians to come forward as social workers and to be involved in frontline care for vulnerable children. But we also need more Christians in politics, who will use their influence to put the needs of children first.

When you interact with your MP, when you vote in an election, how far up the agenda are the needs of widows and orphans on your priority list? Through my work with Home for Good I have had the privilege of speaking with senior politicians about reforming the care system, better supporting looked-after children, and finding ways for the church to be good news for the most vulnerable in our society. Whether it is at a local or a national level, when the church goes to the government with solutions as well as problems, we have more opportunity to make a positive difference.

Work

Some of us have the opportunity to choose the kind of work that we do. Some of us have the opportunity to switch job. One way in which we can serve the purposes of God in the world is to choose our job based on God's priorities for us. Caring for the vulnerable is a key component of many of our jobs. For example, as we have seen, teaching is a frontline care activity. So is working in law, the police service, and, of course, social work.

As we make decisions about our own working life, and also as we influence the decisions of others in our family and church community, how can we help make sure that God is front and centre in our decision-making process? How can we demonstrate the character of God by our choice of career? The question is not whether or not to get involved, whether grace or works is more important, whether Paul or James is our guru of choice, whether we worship God with head or heart, with heart or hands. The question is where we can best enjoy the good works God has prepared for us to do.

There are lots of resources to inspire Christians to care for vulnerable children and to find out how churches can better support foster carers, special guardians, and adoptive parents on the Home for Good website.[20]

Elderly Care

The epistle of James calls us to demonstrate true religion by caring for widows and orphans in their distress. We have explored what this could mean in our day and age to care for orphans. But what about widows?

In the ancient world there was no welfare state, and it was a patriarchal society where lone elderly women faced many challenges just to survive. In our day, the elderly still face many challenges.

Dementia. According to the Alzheimer's Society there are more than 850,000 people in the UK who are suffering from dementia, with numbers set to rise to more than one million by 2025.

- **225,000 will develop dementia this year. That's one every three minutes.**
- **70 per cent of people in care homes have dementia or severe memory problems.**

Though the large majority of people with dementia are elderly, there are also more than 40,000 people under the age of sixty-five with dementia in the UK. For more information visit: www.alzheimers. org.uk.

Loneliness. Did you know that...?

- **17 per cent of older people are in contact with family, friends, and neighbours less than once a week, and 11 per cent are in contact less than once a month.[21]**
- **More than half (51 per cent) of all people aged seventy-five and over live alone (ONS, 2010).**
- **Two-fifths all older people (about 3.9 million) say the television is their main company (Age UK, 2014).**
- **63 per cent of adults aged fifty-two or over who have been widowed, and 51 per cent of the same group who are separated or divorced, report feeling lonely some of the time or often.**
- **59 per cent of adults aged over fifty-two who report poor health say they feel lonely some of the time or often, compared to 21 per cent who say they are in excellent health.**
- **A higher percentage of women than men report feeling lonely some of the time or often.**

It seems that loneliness is more than just social isolation or an emotional response. Some research has shown that loneliness is actually harmful to our health. According to one study, social isolation is a comparable risk factor for early death as smoking fifteen cigarettes a day, and is worse for us than well-known risk factors such as obesity and physical inactivity. Apparently, loneliness can increase the likelihood of mortality by 26 per cent.[22] For more information visit www.campaigntoendloneliness.org.[23]

Practical opportunities. The Reverend Steve Morris of St Cuthbert's Church in North Wembley has been piloting a project that may help with both dementia and loneliness in older people. Steve talks about the project in an article for the website Christian Today,[24] and he goes on to explain:

> I set up a group called day-timers. It was for people who were at home during the day and attracted many people who had been going to church for years. The session started with a person telling us their life story. We gave 20 minutes and each week we heard different tales. Oh, and they were astounding. We heard stories of tragedy and delight. And what was interesting was that these people who had "known" each other for decades had really only known the surface. The storytelling bound us together and that group continues. I liked it because by telling stories we honoured the lives people had lived and affirmed that they had value. So often people simply aren't interested in old people's stories – but we were. In fact, some of the stories were real eye-openers – especially the lovely prim and proper lady who had been a dancer at the Raymond Revue Bar in the 60s. You couldn't make it up.
>
> I get the honour of telling people's stories at their funerals. Many of these are moving and astounding. But I don't want to wait till people have died to tell their stories. I want to know now and celebrate now. In that way, we honour God

who has each and every precious life in the palm of his hands. And so, we move to memory café – our weekly offering to our community. It is a place for people who are forgetting their stories, slowly and inexorably, as Alzheimer's takes hold. We've been listening to people's life tales and recording them, so that when they forget we have them still. We plan an archive – and the stories so far are simply thrilling. But most of all we want to say that stories matter, lives count and what has been is not wasted, not a single bit of it.

There are many practical ways we can care for the elderly in our neighbourhoods.

Why not explore the resources available? Here are just a couple of examples:

- **The Gift of Years Project from BRF seeks to help churches increase the provision of spiritual care services for older people, raise awareness of older people's spiritual needs, and improve skills, knowledge, and confidence within communities in addressing these needs.**[25]
- **The Pilgrim's Friend Society offers resources to help to deliver cognitive and spiritual stimulation for older people, including those with early-stage dementia, in a social setting that is fun and engaging.**[26]

FUSION

We have seen that we don't have to pick sides between James and Paul. But in seeking to reconcile these two great biblical authors we must not fail to hear James' challenge to us to consider whether our faith is real or not, based not just on what we believe or even who we believe in. James challenges us to see our faith worked out in our lives and in concert with the rest of Scripture. One of the litmus tests of the authenticity of our profession of faith is the practice of our faith through compassionate service to the poor and vulnerable. James calls us to the bravery of faithful service to God through our willingness to care for the "widows and orphans" as anything else. Will you respond to the call?

Further Reading

Krish and Miriam Kandiah, *Home for Good* (Hodder, 2014)

Christine Pohl, *Making Room* (Eerdmans, 1999)

Krish Kandiah, *God is Stranger* (Hodder, 2017)

Dan Cruver (ed), *Reclaiming Adoption* (CreateSpace Independent Publishing Platform, 2010)

Ralph P. Martin, *Word Biblical Commentary on James* (Thomas Nelson, 2010)

Douglas Moo, *Tyndale Commentary on James* (revised edition, IVP, 2015)

R. T. Kendall, "Works" in *Justification by Works: How Works Vindicate True Faith: Sermons on James 1–3* (Paternoster, 2002)

Steve Morris, *Memory Café: How to Engage with Memory Loss and Build Community* (Grove Books, 2017)

Testimony from Fiona, 55, Plymouth

I feel brave when I know Jesus is with me. He is the one who makes me strong. Often in my work I have to confront people in difficult situations and I feel God's strength just at the right time. For example, when I have two drug addicts at each another's throats and I have to intervene.

I have had a lot of challenges in my life. Surviving an abusive upbringing was a big one. The abuse was both physical and mental. I had to rebuild my self-worth after the trauma of rape at an early age and having a voice that could not be heard. I left a broken home and had to learn to believe in myself. One big challenge was training as a Christian counsellor and, through that process, facing my past and a lot of what happened, including the challenges of not being afraid of touch and learning the right way to express myself physically and appropriately. There is also the ongoing calling of standing up for others who are struggling. This includes accepting love and the everyday challenge of reaching out to others and finding ways of helping them be loved and accepted.

I have learned the hard way to take these challenges through trying and having counselling. Working through and learning that my identity is in Jesus, not in what has happened to me or what I might have done, I talk to God about everything. I learned to face my shame and realized that it was not all my fault and, with the help of others and God, I learned to love myself. And through this I can share it with others. It's taken a lot of time to get where I am. I had people around me who had faith in me, and this helped, especially my husband, who I met when I was seventeen.

Also, when I was sixteen and my parents had split up, I lived with my grandfather. My father was gay and we often had his partners live with us, and when not he would beat us, so when they split I went to live with my grandfather. When he died, a young, newlywed couple from the local church took me to live with them and tried to help me. This is why I run the Greenhouse Project – to help others. I believe because of my past and the love shown to me, I want to do the same for others, and God has given me the skills and love to do this.

Jesus has changed my life. He saved me. He gave me hope and made me brave. He gave me the will to live when things seemed hopeless, and He gave me self-worth through others. I would not be BRAVE without him.

MEET SIM DENDY: interview by Krish Kandiah

What's the bravest thing you have ever seen?

Having been a retained firefighter in West Sussex for ten years, I saw many things that would traditionally be considered brave – people rescuing cats from trees, people being cut out of cars, and families escaping from homes on fire in the middle of the night. But the bravest thing I have ever seen was my wife, Lottie, giving birth to our children. Bravery is all about knowing that what you are about to do will cause you pain but doing it anyway. So my wife must be very brave – she gave birth four times in total!

Sim, who were the people that helped you come to faith?

I had the privilege of Christian parents and being brought up in church (well, my dad was the pastor so we had little choice whether we went or not!), but the most significant people in my journey to faith were definitely my Sunday school teachers. I have some great memories of these heroes who, every week, often in unsuitable, tiny, damp rooms at the back of the church, would invest in my young life by unlocking the mysteries of God and His incredible Word. I will always be grateful for the part they played in my life, and I now look for any opportunity to thank those who do the same today for my kids.

When you were younger, who were the people that helped you take discipleship seriously?

When I left school at eighteen I went to work for my local church as a children's and schools worker. Each week I met with Tony, one of the church leaders, who would sit with me and go through my diary for the week ahead and ask me what I was reading, what I was spending my money on, who I was praying for, how my relationship with my future wife Lottie was going, and so on. That weekly routine formed healthy habits in my life that I still do today. The other person who discipled me at that same time was Dave, another church leader who also worked for the church as a community worker. He taught me to love people the way Jesus did, that each person has value and deserves our attention. We never sat down and talked face to face unless it was over a pub lunch. It was always through simple conversation as we set up after-school clubs, took children to football matches, or helped people with limited ability fill in their forms. This was side-by-side discipleship that shaped the way I lived and loved.

I loved visiting your local church. What do you think is the role of the local church in disciple making?

Thanks, Krish. We loved having you visit Freedom Church – come again soon!

I think the church has everything to do with disciple making – it is the great commission. However, it is not just the responsibility of the church (the organization) to disciple, but the people who make up the church family themselves to disciple those around them. Sometimes people make the mistake of thinking the church pastor, minister, elders, or youth leaders should be the only ones to disciple new believers, or that the church office should organize a ten-week discipleship programme to aid them in their personal development. It is the responsibility of the WHOLE church, each individual member of the body, to make determined disciples of ourselves and others at any moment of our day, even when it is inconvenient – when we sit in our home, when we walk down the road, when we go to bed and when we get up (Deuteronomy 6:7).

How have members of your congregation shown bravery in recent years?

We have just partnered with Christians Against Poverty (CAP) for a Debt Centre to help set people free from often complex financial situations. We have an amazing team of volunteer befrienders who regularly visit their clients, take them shopping, reorganize their finances, and support their families. One has even given short-term lodgings in their home. They literally do anything they can to help. But sometimes, after all this love, kindness, and energy has been spent on them, the client decides not to continue on the difficult road to becoming debt free and walks away from the process. I have watched this happen a few times and am always impressed by the way that these befrienders take a breath, smile, and carry on looking for others to help – that's brave.

If you could have one phrase carved on your gravestone, what would it be?

Sim was here, now he's gone.
He made a difference, one by one.

TAME IT!

SIM DENDY

If you are wise and understand God's ways, prove it by living an honorable life, doing good works with the humility that comes from wisdom.

James 3:13 (NLT)

I can remember my words as if they were being played at full volume in high-quality surround sound. I was standing in the queue in a coffee shop, happily minding my own business, waiting for the opportunity to order my regular flat white coffee, when a small child came up to me, stuck his tongue out, and blew a raspberry. Having four children of my own, I was used to the most unexpected things being part of everyday life. I started talking to him: asked his name, how old was he, where his mum was, and so on, but he just kept blowing raspberries. Eventually, in a bit of exasperation and trying to be humorous, I said to this little boy, "I have children and they can be a bit of a nightmare sometimes, like you." As soon as I said it I felt terrible. Yes, he had started to get a little annoying (and seriously, where was his mum?!), but I was meant to be the adult in this ad hoc interaction and I could have chosen my words so much better, or said nothing at all. But the words were out of my mouth before I could stop them. Something I still regret.

Benjamin Zander, the long-time conductor of the Boston Philharmonic Orchestra and author of *Art of Possibility*, told the following story in his TED Talk from 2008:

I learned this from a woman who survived Auschwitz, one of the rare survivors. She went to Auschwitz when she was fifteen years old, her brother was eight, and the parents were lost. And she told me this. She said, "We were on the train going to Auschwitz and I looked down and saw my brother's shoes were missing. I said, 'Why are you so stupid, can't you keep your things together for goodness' sake?'" The way an elder sister might speak to a younger brother. Unfortunately, it was the last thing she ever said to him because she never saw him again. He did not survive. And so, when she came out of Auschwitz, she made a vow. She told me this. She said, "I walked out of Auschwitz into life and I made a vow. And the vow was, I will never say anything that couldn't stand as the last thing I ever say.[27]

In light of this:

- Have you ever said something you regret?
- What if our last words to someone really were the last words they would ever hear?
- Would it change the way we spoke?

James 3:1

Krish has just inspired us through the words of James 2 to "live it" out in our faith and our works, to be active disciples who are doing, not just talking. It seems a little back to front that in chapter 3 James then challenges us in what we say and the heart from which our words overflow.

As disciples of Jesus, and with even more emphasis if we teach others, one of the most important lessons to learn is how we use our words. Words can lift people up and inspire them to greatness, but words can also crush people's ambitions and desires (Ephesians 4:29).

In his third chapter, James addresses "taming the tongue" by challenging us in verse 10 to stop cursing and praising from the same mouth. This is a little confusing as he has just said in verse 8 that no human being can tame the tongue. Though the concept is simple, the discipline to *tame it* is not easy. As determined disciples of Jesus, how can we train ourselves to be wise with the words that we speak and when we choose to speak them?

HEAD: DOES SIZE REALLY MATTER?

Have you ever been the designated person at a social event to offer the freshly cut slices of cake dripping with icing? The responses we receive are often along the lines of, "I shouldn't really, but go on then…" or, "I suppose you only live once!" or my favourite: "I guess I've been good recently." Why do we know in our head that we are doing is not always for our best, but we still choose to go ahead anyway?

And for what it's worth, I love a bit of cake. After all, I have been good recently!

Small is Powerful (James 3:1-6)

James gives us powerful images in chapter 3 of a number of small things that can make a huge difference. A rider can control his horse, regardless of the size of the horse, using only a small bit that fits into the horse's mouth. In the same way, a small rudder can force a large ship to turn whichever way the captain chooses. And a large-scale forest fire can destroy everything in its path, having started with the smallest of sparks.

If James had written his letter today, he probably would have added the mobile phone to his list. That such a small device can carry great power is evident in our daily lives. Did you know that the mobile phone you carry in your pocket today has greater processing power than the computer operated by thousands of IBM engineers to land Apollo 11 on the moon almost fifty years ago?[28]

But it is not the technical power of our phone that is so dangerous; it is how we choose to use it. With one phone call, one tweet, one inappropriate selfie, one unkind video, one Instagram image, or one Facebook post, we can have an immediate, worldwide impact. That in the wrong hands could be catastrophic.

Likewise, the tongue is small but very powerful and requires appropriate control. James used the tongue as an example throughout chapter 3, but we have to take care of more than just the words that come out of our mouths. We must also be careful with our pen, computer keyboard, or texting fingers.

We each carry an enormous amount of power, and our responsibility as part of discipleship is to learn to live like Jesus did and mirror Him.

Both the Old Testament prophets and the Gospel writers talked about Jesus and the way He would choose His words carefully.

He was oppressed and afflicted,
yet he did not open his mouth;
he was led like a lamb to the slaughter,
and as a sheep before its shearers is silent,
so he did not open his mouth.

Isaiah 53:7

Then the high priest stood up before them and asked Jesus,
"Are you not going to answer? What is this testimony that
these men are bringing against you?" But Jesus remained silent
and gave no answer.

Mark 14:60–61

Jesus often chose to stay silent, but He also knew the right moment to speak out. He understood when a kind word was needed and when gentle remonstration would be required. He knew, whenever a crowd gathered, when it was time to give a key address that would be remembered for all time and when it was the right time to withdraw and spend time with His Father. Jesus was always mindful of the moment. Conversely, we often feel obliged to deliver whatever the crowd around us wants to hear.

Both a timely word and a gentle silence can be powerful. Learning when to speak and when to keep our mouths closed is an ongoing discipline.

You are Powerful

There is power in each one of us to influence those around us. We truly can make a difference. Throughout history it has often been one voice, one moment, one vote, one act that has changed the world.

The Muhlenberg legend[29] is an urban myth that claims it was by only one vote that the new settlers in the recently discovered land of America chose to speak English rather than German. Although there is a record of a petition put forward by German immigrants that was rejected by one vote in 1794 for some proposed translation laws, the Muhlenberg legend has since become a routine story often used by politicians to encourage voters that their votes count. Though many historians dismiss this as a myth, it is a powerful statement all the same. History is clear that it was one act of defiance by Rosa Parks on a bus in Alabama that reignited a struggling Civil Rights movement. This was followed by 250,000 people marching to listen to the famous speech by Martin Luther King, Jr on the steps of the Lincoln Memorial in Washington, and a nation was transformed.[30]

Rosa Parks was only one person, but she made a significant difference, not as a loud extrovert shouting from a platform but from being determined and quietly brave. Susan Cain the author says of her:

> *I had always imagined Rosa Parks as a stately woman with a bold temperament, someone who could easily stand up to a busload of glowering passengers. But when she died in 2005 at the age of ninety-two, the flood of obituaries recalled her as soft-spoken, sweet, and small in stature. They said she was "timid and shy" but had "the courage of a lion." They were full of phrases like "radical humility" and "quiet fortitude."[31]*

One is an influential number, and each one of us has the capacity to realize that we have great potential to influence those around us for good. We have an opportunity to consider how we shape this potential and use it to the greater good. In a speech Winston Churchill gave in the House of Commons in 1906, he said: "Where there is great power there is great responsibility." Or, as Jesus put it in Luke 12:48, "From everyone who has been given much, much will be demanded."

How can we handle this great responsibility?

Learn How to Tame It (James 3:7-12)...

A few months ago, our family experienced a once-in-a-lifetime holiday to Florida. As we are a large family with four children, I never thought this would ever be possible, but through the unbelievable generosity of several kind friends, we were able to spend two wonderful weeks together in the Sunshine State. While we were there we visited some of the incredible theme parks on offer. SeaWorld is a venue that is known because of its family of killer whales, which are the main feature of the park. As parents we were feeling a little uncomfortable, not sure whether we should go and see the show or not, but our curiosity overcame us and we took our seats along with thousands of others around this huge tank of water. The show that followed was spectacular. We watched these beautiful animals swim, jump, and perform tricks with strength and agility that was inspiring.

What is it that impresses us so much about seeing a trained animal at work? Whether it is a horse and rider completing their dressage routine in the Summer Olympics, a group of chimpanzees enacting a tea party, or Pudsey the dog becoming the first animal to win *Britain's Got Talent*, we seem to be fascinated – and sometimes horrified – by the ability of human beings to tame animals.

In verse 7 of James 3 we are reminded that people have been able to tame a variety of animals (so this is not a modern phenomenon), but we can't tame the tongue in the same way. I don't know how you train a killer whale to jump on demand, but it has been achieved. I don't know how you get a dog to perform on a stage in front of four judges on a live TV show, but it has been done. James concurs that such incredible feats are impressive, but we won't be able to do the same for the tongue, which is a "restless evil, full of deadly poison" (James 3:8).

It seems as though James is underlining this important point, as he has already challenged us in verse 2 of this chapter that "if we could control our tongues, we would be perfect and could also control ourselves in *every* other way" (James 3:2, NLT) [emphasis mine]. James sees this aspect of discipline as essential to the whole person becoming more like Jesus; if we could just grapple with the things we say and overcome some of our wayward comments. this would have implications on our whole understanding of personal discipleship.

...But Still Retain It (James 3:13)

It is imperative that this power we carry in our use, or misuse, of the tongue is brought under control. We come under God's authority and bring our everyday strengths under His control, our inbuilt nature under His discipline. God does not want us to lose this power. He gave it to us in the first place – created in His image, as we were – but He wants us to bring it under control and use it for good. This is wisdom. Wisdom to know when to say something and when not to.

Verse 13 begins to unpack this concept of wisdom and the difference between human and Godly wisdom. It intrigues me that James was suggesting that if we are wise and understand God's ways we should be doing good works with the "humility that comes from wisdom". This word "humility" is sometimes translated as "gentleness" and comes from the Greek *prautés*, from the root word *praus*, which is translated as "meek".

Power under authority, strength under control, nature under discipline. This word *praus* was borrowed from the military of the time and relates to how a war horse would be trained. The Greek army would find the wildest horses in the mountains and bring them home to be broken in. After months of training they sorted the horses into categories: some were discarded, some had been broken and were useful for bearing burdens, others were useful for ordinary duty, and the fewest of all graduated as war horses.

When a horse passed the conditioning required to be a war horse, its state was described as *praus*. The war horse had power under authority, strength under control. A war horse never ceased to be determined, strong, and passionate. However, it had learned to bring its nature under discipline. It stopped being wild, unruly, out of control, and rebellious. A war horse had learned to bring that nature under control without losing its strength or resilience. It would now respond to the slightest touch of the rider, stand in the face of the advancing enemy, thunder into battle, and stop at a whisper.

It was now *praus*, or "meek".

Power under Authority

When I was much younger, I lived in the Fens in the east of England. It is a beautiful part of the country on the banks of the River Ouse. As a child, I never fully appreciated what was all around me. My neighbours had a farm and kept horses; I was allowed to help exercise and ride them each day as long as I also helped to "muck them out". Although this was probably fair payment, on hot and smelly days it was not my idea of fun.

On one occasion my neighbour, Audrey Sarkis, visited a horse auction and purchased a young foal that she decided to break in herself, something she had never done before. This young animal was wild and wouldn't let any of us go anywhere near her at first. But each day the family would take turns to spend time near her stall, talking to her, whistling, feeding her from a distance, and giving her time to calm down and get to know them.

After a visit to the local library, they came home with an armful of books about how to "break in" a horse (the internet hadn't been invented back then, and watching YouTube videos or reading a blog on Horse Breaking for Dummies wasn't an option). The thing I recall most is how long it took.

Often they would take this horse into the training ring, a round patch of grass surrounded by a makeshift wooden fence held together by orange binding twine, to try to encourage the horse to walk in a circle while one of my neighbours held on to a long rope. More often than not, it seemed to me, as an easily bored ten-year-old spectator, that the training session would end in disarray with the horse, who was called Lady, often acting like anything other than a lady or gentleman. After many months of frothing, panting, and kicking (and that was just my neighbours) Lady eventually accepted a saddle, a bit and a rider. That first official ride on her back was a great time of celebration after months of hard work.

Through that experience, I saw first hand that to tame a horse to give up its natural instincts is extremely challenging. I can only imagine that to tame a horse and retain its natural, inbuilt, determined, wild strength is an even more challenging process.

But that is what James writes about in this chapter: to tame the power that we each have and to bring it under control. That the very same natural, inbuilt, and determined wild strength remains, but now we have the wisdom to know when to utilize it and when not to.

Paradox of James

Throughout this chapter there appears to be a repeating tension between different truths that seem to challenge one another. They are exact opposites – a paradox.

James wrote using paradoxical statements here to intrigue us and question our normal thinking. A paradox is simply two things that seem to be opposites but are completely true at the same time. For example, when we say "less is more". The statement uses two opposite words that appear to contradict one another, but the concept behind this phrase is that something minimal or *less* complicated often has a greater impact or is *more* appreciated. A paradox.

James begins by saying that taming the tongue will bring perfection (verse 2) and then he goes on to say that it cannot be done (verse 8). He argues that the tongue is restless, sometimes praising God and in the next instant cursing those who have been made in His image (verse 9). How can this be?

He suggests that it is like a bubbling spring providing both fresh and salty water, or a fig tree producing olives (verses 11–12). t is simply not possible.

The idea of setting an aspiring personal target is not a new idea. Every advertising campaign for a new product does that, but rarely does the same commercial throw doubt on to this suggested vision of perfection.

Imagine if a fitness company were to bring a new fitness machine to market with an advert that says if you buy this latest piece of fitness equipment and use it regularly it will make you fit. You can have your dream body with very little effort and for a lot less than it costs to have gym membership.

Sounds ideal?

But what if the advertisement then goes on to say that, in all honesty, it probably won't work. Actually, they tell you that people tried to get fit using this new product and most people gave up after a few weeks. Their product required too much effort and discipline, so instead of persisting with the training regime they tucked the said item in the under-stairs cupboard or sold it on eBay instead.

Would you buy one?

This is what James is saying. Be careful what you say, but all the best with that as no one has ever done it before. He implies that only God has true wisdom sorted out and He isn't prepared to make it available as a free download just at this moment.

It requires more than just work and determined discipleship to tame it; we require the Holy Spirit, our comforter and helper to walk alongside us. True wisdom only comes from above.

True Wisdom (James 3:13–18)

Would you consider yourself wise? What about your neighbour? Are they wise? Or a parent in the playground? Or the person behind the till at the local supermarket? Who do we go to for wise counsel or sound advice?

A new phenomenon has been emerging recently, often called "wisdom of the crowd". It is a fascinating concept in a world that is becoming increasingly individualistic. People now turn to the crowd, often in an online forum, rather than a knowledgeable expert, for advice on what to do next.

We used to have agony aunt columns in newspapers and magazines, or with regular slots on daytime television. Then those were no longer fashionable and seen as a bit of a joke, with made-up questions and celebrity "agony aunts" (such as singer James Blunt answering people's grave concerns in *Metro*[32]). These days, apparently, the wisdom is to be found among the masses. For example, the novel *The Lord of the Rings* was voted by the public as the greatest piece of literature written in the twentieth century, which must be true because the anonymous crowd said so.[33] An instance of "wisdom of the crowd" being taken as truth, regardless of some literary experts' opinions to the contrary.

All this wisdom can sound plausible in itself. But when we scratch the surface we find that it is shallow and self-benefiting. James (the saint, not Blunt) calls us to seek the wisdom of heaven. In his writing, he tells us there are two types of wisdom; the one we choose will determine the direction of our life and the consequences of our actions.

James, with great timing, provided for us this paradoxical challenge: to be careful with our tongues as determined disciples while at the same time being aware that this is a near-impossible task. James concludes by pointing us back to God himself, the only source of true wisdom.

Earthly Wisdom (James 3:13–16)

As someone who regularly preaches a message on Sundays, I am always challenged by how I live out my well-rehearsed, thought-through, and prayed-through presentation on a Monday. Our heavenly wisdom is only as good as our earthly activity – or, as Krish put it in the previous chapter, "the good works God has prepared for us to do". The fruit that James writes about at the end of chapter 3 is the result of that wisdom. If we rely on earthly wisdom, then the fruit of that will be to "harbour bitter envy or selfish ambition in [our] hearts", which will create "disorder and every evil practice".

James even describes our attempts to manage ourselves as earthly, unspiritual, and even demonic.

Godly Wisdom (James 3:17)

"But the wisdom that comes from heaven is first of all pure; then peace-loving, considerate, submissive, full of mercy and good fruit, impartial and sincere" (James 3:17). What a different list to his criticism of our earthly wisdom! Godly wisdom comes from heaven and will be known by its fruit.

Matthew 7 reminds us that we can tell false prophets by their fruit (verse 16) because, of course, a "good tree bears good fruit, but a bad tree bears bad fruit" (verse 17). If we want to be people of good fruit, it is important that we stay continuously connected to heaven, ensuring that we are listening to God and His wisdom, before we open our mouths to provide our poorer version of earthly wisdom.

Godly wisdom leads to control. It is the bit that controls the horse, the rudder that controls the ship. If we let God and His wisdom control our words, it will shape our direction.

And the Result is... (James 3:18)

Fruit! If we are truly wise then the fruit will always be good. In the final verse of this challenging chapter, where fruit is referenced in verses 12 and 17, James finishes with a great reward. If we stay connected to heaven and ensure we are following the wisdom of God, we will receive the fruit of being peace-loving.

Peacekeepers use words to avoid conflict; peacemakers use words to prevent conflict. Those who "sow in peace will reap a harvest of righteousness". There is a reward for the challenge of watching what we say, and it is righteousness – simply being right in God's eyes.

- If small things can make such a big difference, what small things are you feeling prompted to put into place to make a big impact? Make one small change in your home or workplace and see if anyone notices.

- We all carry greatness within us, but what can we do to develop our "meekness" without losing anything of God's power that we carry?

- Who are you looking to for your wisdom? The internet, podcasts, books, or magazines? Find someone you trust – a church leader, small group leader, a Christian friend – and ask to meet up regularly to make yourself accountable. It will be well worth the price of a coffee.

HEART: WHAT IS THE SOUND ON THE INSIDE?

There is a tension between extremes that we try to hold together. For instance, how do we remain *in* the world but not *of* the world (John 15:19)? How can we sing our songs to God one moment and be angered by a slow driver in front of us the next – out of the same mouth praising and cursing?

Matthew 15:18 reminds us that "the things that come out of a person's mouth come from the heart." If we want to change what comes out of our mouth, then the change must begin in our heart. Improving our hidden attitudes will affect how we communicate with those around us.

Paul faced the challenge of doing what he didn't want to do (Romans 7:15) and talked about the thorn in his flesh (2 Corinthians 12:7), which some suggest may have been a habit he was trying to overcome. Similarly, discipleship is about getting hold of our weaker spiritual habits and intentionally making changes.

Is it possible to change what is inherent within us? James suggests in verse 8 that no human can tame their tongue; it is only possible with God's help.

Heart as an Indicator

My car has a digital fuel indicator which tells me how many miles are left in the tank. I started driving decades ago when everything was black and white, petrol at the pump was 50p a litre, and the fuel gauge was notorious for being inaccurate when you were going up or down a hill. Digital gauges fascinate me. I have no idea how they work, but they seem to be incredibly accurate and consistent. The downside is that, to my wife's frustration, I see no reason to fill up until the indicator tells me that we have fewer than five miles left in the tank. The garage is only a mile from our house and so I am normally confident that we will be fine. So far, I have no embarrassing mishaps to reveal!

Similarly, how we speak and what we say is an indicator of the state of our heart. We are often shocked when people close to us, whom we love dearly, say terrible things when they are tired, under stress, or angry about something.

Several years ago, we found out that one of our children often came home from school and said things to their siblings that were unkind. We tried to understand the source of the behaviour. We tried correcting them with various schemes of reward and punishment but nothing seemed to work. One day we gave them a small snack when we picked them up from school and the difference was incredible. They had simply been hungry, and their behaviour was an indicator of their hunger. Needless to say, after-school snacks became a regular feature in our home.

A useful tool to becoming more self-aware is known by the acronym HALT: Hungry, Angry, Lonely, Tired. It is a simple concept that helps us understand that when these basic needs are not met, we are susceptible to unhealthy behaviours and reactions that we might later regret.

Our tongue, if not HALTed, often exposes the frustration that is taking place inside of us, emotions that whirl around when we feel we have been wronged in some way. On a good day we can control unnecessary outbursts, but on a bad day, or, ironically, in supposedly "safe" company, such as our family where we feel secure and comfortable, we can unleash words that can never be caught in mid-air and edited before they are heard.

> *Three things that never come back: the spent arrow; the spoken word; the lost opportunity.*
>
> **William George Plunkett**[34]

With online comments being encouraged in real time, things can often be typed without pause for thought. When read out of context or on another day, these can be deeply damaging and completely inappropriate.

We talked earlier about the power of smartphones which now have social media apps readily available to young people. These encourage immediate conversation using a photo or selfie that reveals their present activity which, in theory, only exists temporarily. In reality, there have been situations of young people sending inappropriate images to one another that have been copied and then sent around school groups and friends, causing enormous embarrassment or, tragically, much worse.

Once again, these simple and immediate actions reveal something of the heart. Why would someone choose to say unkind things in a moment of hunger, anger, loneliness, or tiredness? Is there any truth behind the verbal tirade? Why would someone send a picture that they would never show to their parents to an online friend they have never met in person? What is going on inside their heart that causes them to reach out to a stranger in such a way? James recognizes that we all make "many mistakes", but if we could only control our tongue then we could be perfect and control ourselves in every other way (verse 2, NLT).

This is a great challenge that comes with a great reward. If we can get this speaking the right thing at the right time under control, then we will see other aspects of our life align themselves as well. Surely it is worth pursuing. But what comes first: the words we say or the feelings we control inside? Determined in our quest to become more like Jesus, we endeavour to develop all areas simultaneously.

James encourages us to take every word captive before it is spoken, but the Apostle Paul goes one step further. In 2 Corinthians 10:5 (NIV), he encourages the early church to "take captive every thought to make it obedient to Christ".

The learning cycle that exists here is endless. We determine to train our hearts and harness our thoughts to ensure that they are noble, pure, lovely, and admirable (Philippians 4:8). This will then impact our speech, be it verbal or written. At the same time, if we train ourselves to pause before we say something we might regret, this will also impact our heart and the way that we feel.

In my role as a church leader for a number of years, I have sometimes received a Monday morning – often lengthy – email from a member of the church raising "concern" about the volume of the worship time, the quality of the preacher, or the standard of the Communion wine. Sadly, through many defensive and rash responses that I should never have sent, I have learned to implement systems to protect my heart and to protect others. Now when I have an awkward email to write, I often check it first with my wife or a colleague. What seems obvious to me in my desire to correct someone or to take correction myself can change when I obtain a different perspective on what might really be happening within the exchange of emails.

Another tactic I use when I need to send challenging correspondence is to sleep on it. Not literally, of course (I don't print off the email and put it under my pillow), but I give myself a few hours and then look at it again. It is amazing how different things can look in the morning when you are fully awake. Last – and my personal preference – is to go and see the person and have a careful conversation. So many things can be misunderstood through written messages, whether they be emails, tweets, text messages, or Facebook comments, even with the use of emojis. Face-to-face conversations are always best to get to the bottom of concerns being raised. The phrase about our eyes being the "window to the soul", loosely based around Matthew 6:22, is true when we engage in challenging conversations with people. If we are able to look them in the eye, we are likely to better understand the heart behind the words being said.

On one occasion (I have a lot of personal experiences around this topic that I would love to forget) I was upset with a member of staff who had not completed the tasks he had been set and I needed some important information for a meeting I was about to attend. In my frustration, I marched down the corridor toward his office with every intention of throwing open the door and demanding to have this report that with every passing minute was growing more and more urgent. Fortunately, just as I reached his office door, with steam emitting from my ears, another colleague passed by and said to me, "Did you know his mum passed away at the weekend?" What great timing. Instantly humbled, I took my hand off the door handle and walked away, knowing that I had come incredibly close to saying something I would have deeply regretted. If I am honest, I even regret the fact that I made so many assumptions and didn't find out more before coming to my own conclusion.

Reflection

In Lisa's chapter, we considered how James uses the metaphor of the man who glances in a mirror and then forgets what he looks like. In the same way, in our busy world, many of us never truly stop and reflect on the day that we have just had, nor on what we could have said or done better as determined disciples.

It is generally considered that we learn through experience, but in my personal understanding as a church pastor, this is not automatically true. People don't always learn through their experiences. It is not uncommon for an issue that they struggled with previously to come back round again with some regularity, season by season. In truth, we are more likely to learn through assessed experience. This is a key element to our determined discipleship – to be both intentional in our thought and deliberate in our action. We look at who we are becoming and see what needs to be improved. For example, if you want to become a faster runner, you time yourself and endeavour to improve on it. If we never assess our progress, we will never be sure if we are improving or getting worse. In this area of personal and determined discipleship, we develop the habit of regularly reflecting on what we have said and whether people have understood what was meant. This can be achieved on our own as part of our daily diet of reading the Bible, journalling, and prayer each day. It can also be helpful to talk things through with a close friend.

On more than one occasion, my wife Lottie has had to have a Sunday lunchtime conversation with me around something I said as part of my talk in church that morning. Often it is a one-line joke or an off-the-cuff remark that is deemed unhelpful or unnecessary. My typical reaction is initially defensive, but with Lottie's track record of being right 99.9 per cent of the time, I eventually end up agreeing with her. On a couple of occasions, I have even had to call our technical team on a Sunday afternoon and ask them to edit or delete the recording before it is added to the church podcast ready for download. I have so much more learning to do in this area. My prepared words are fine, but my ad hoc, "trying hard to be funny because I want to be liked", comments still reveal something of my heart. I am full of good intentions but require further training and more determined discipleship.

Proverbs 17:28 reminds us that even fools, if they remain silent, will seem wise. How many times do we wish we had said nothing and just listened? If only I had paused and thought for a few more seconds. Reflection is the opportunity to rewind the day and go through conversations and moments when we have blurted something out without really thinking through the value of our words and whether they will be helpful to the individual or group we are talking to.

Consistency

Many years ago, I was working in an open-plan office for a printing company. I was responsible for a number of large national accounts, ensuring that their printing requests were processed, printed, and delivered on time. Because of the open-plan office layout, I could hear everyone's conversations, from their business phone calls to what they watched on the telly the previous night. After I had been there a few weeks and was beginning to get my head round the new job, a colleague from the factory came to see me. He told me that I probably hadn't realized it but the office had changed since I had arrived. Apparently, it had been to be a difficult place to work, with regular arguments, inappropriate jokes, and a lot of swearing. However, since I had started it had changed – or I think, more likely, people went to the staff room and had a moan there instead. What intrigued me most about that comment was that I had never announced to my colleagues that I didn't swear or participate in gossip. I just tried to ensure that my behaviour was consistent.

One of the things James is challenging us to do in this chapter, especially for those who teach, is to develop our consistency through perseverance. To speak well of someone for one moment is easy. To be consistent in what we say *all* the time is so much more challenging. Teachers and preachers, what we say on a Sunday can be ruined by our actions on a Monday. The wisdom James talks about is one of an attitude that lasts all week, doing good works with humility, not just looking good in front of a crowd on a Sunday. If I am not consistent in the home, my children are often the first to remind me of what I said at church, with frustratingly perfect recollection.

Love Wisdom

Part of training the heart and discovering our God-given wisdom is reflecting on our activities and daily language with consistency. It is also important, however, that we consider what we are putting into our lives. With such a variety of easily accessible technology, it is very easy to fill our time and minds with conflicting noise. When I was a child, we didn't have a television, as my dad was concerned that it was a time waster and believed it would not be good to fill our minds with the depravity that the existing three channels and the recent addition of a fourth channel (creatively named Channel 4) would offer between the hours of 6 a.m. and midnight. (Do you remember the test card image with the girl playing noughts and crosses before we had twenty-four-hour television?) I used to visit my neighbour in the week to watch *Dallas*, and then at the weekend I would visit another friend to watch the sports show *Grandstand* with Des Lynam, and the original *The A-Team*. Looking back, I believe my Dad was right about *Dallas*. Now my family sit at home with numerous devices that can access the vast array of information on the internet, and a digital TV with hundreds of channels with the ability to stream iPlayer and Netflix at the push of a button or two. Always available, any time, day or night.

There is so much information available to us that it can be hard to know what to give our attention to. But James says that "the wisdom that comes from heaven is… pure" (verse 17). The world may suggest that if we want to be wise, we should sign up and complete a programme of education in our preferred subject. But pure wisdom comes from God. Not that we shouldn't seek to improve our knowledge and understanding, but this does not replace godly wisdom. Spending time with God and allowing Him to fill our lives with His wisdom brings lasting change, first to our own lives and then to the lives of others.

Godly wisdom is responding to the challenges of our thought life with His perspective and timing. We can only learn this as we spend time in His presence, regularly allowing Him to change us from deep within. There is no easy fix; there is no sign-up to a six-week training programme that we can download from YouTube. If we want to shape our heart to be more like God's, then let us commit to becoming determined disciples and to spending time with Him, allowing His wisdom and love to infiltrate our thinking.

Personally, I find that the challenge of shaping of my heart is an intentional activity that does not happen by accident. It truly is a discipline. I encourage you to find a suitable time and a space that works for you. Some people have a special room or a chair they sit in and have time with God; some people prefer to get out of the house and go for a walk or a drive or a run as they pray and reflect. Find what works and create a pattern and a routine for your life. Try it for a week without telling anyone and see if anyone notices the difference.

Our words create the culture we want to inhabit. They are the clothes that our thoughts wear, they are the wardrobe of our inner life, the outer evidence of our inner reality. If our words come from our heart, then it is worth spending time investing in our heart so that our words reflect more accurately the pure wisdom that comes from God above.

- Write Philippians 4:8 on the inside of your front door so that it is the last thing you see as you head out for the day ahead. Use it as a guide to consider before you speak – a virtual checklist. Am I about to say something that is:

    - True
    - Noble
    - Right
    - Pure
    - Lovely
    - Admirable
    - Excellent
    - Praiseworthy

- What are you drawing from in making decisions? Keep a chart or a diary for a week and see how much time you spend on social media, watching box sets, reading your Bible, listening to podcasts, sleeping, eating, shopping. Make it into a fun exercise, not to make yourself feel guilty but to discover what you are putting your time and energy into and what is therefore feeding your thinking?

- Spend one hour without speaking. Not a single word out loud. What did you learn about yourself?

- Make yourself a cup of tea and sit in your favourite chair. Take some time to write down areas of your thought life that require HALTing or being taken captive (2 Corinthians 10:5) and then pray into them. Maybe this could become a regular part of your time with God?

HANDS: THE FORGOTTEN FRUIT?

James set a huge challenge to watch what we say, which is easy to write but much harder to achieve. If you have ever had a child try to complete a sponsored silence for a few hours, you will know how difficult it is to control the tongue in such a simple exercise as saying nothing.

According to Tom Wright, the description in James is a "country within a country".[35] It is one member among many but it thinks it is better and more important than it is. Over the years, I have had the opportunity to attend and speak at various conferences in the United States of America. Often these trips have been to the State of Texas, where I have a number of friends. Texas is known as the Lone Star State, reflecting its original status as a republic. But there is also a national joke, seemingly supported by many Texans, that they like to be called the Nation of Texas. It's as if they are a country within a country. The tongue, which the writer of James describes here, is no more important than the other members of the body listed by Paul in 1 Corinthians 12, but it thinks it is better than the other members and wants to do its own thing. The tongue, although it is small and has no priority over the other members, has an inordinate amount of power that can have a devastating effect on the other members.

Determined discipleship is intentional. We have to *do* something. Put it into action. Reading this book but making no adjustments in your daily activities is no different from the "mirror glancer" that Lisa mentions in the opening section. But whose advice do we follow? As touched on earlier, the world is awash with wisdom, but the writer of James suggests that the world's wisdom is earthly, unspiritual, and even demonic (verse 15). The wisdom of verse 17 is required here, the kind of wisdom that "comes from heaven". This is godly wisdom, and it outshines earthly wisdom each day before we have even had our breakfast.

The Importance of Self-Control

Godly wisdom leads to control. Taming the tongue requires control. Determined discipleship is all about taking deliberate control of our life, placing it into the safe hands of our Father God, and utilizing his heavenly wisdom. One of the least talked about fruits of the Holy Spirit is self-control.

I have often spoken at weddings on 1 Corinthians 13: "Love is patient, love is kind. It does not envy, it does not boast, it is not proud," and the attributes of love and faithfulness. I have sung many a worship song about joy and peace. In speaking to members of my church who are facing personal challenges, I encourage them to be full of kindness, gentleness, goodness, and patience. But I have never preached to a freshly wed couple on their wedding day about the importance of self-control. I don't think I have heard a Tim Hughes anthem that encourages our congregations to lift their voices in song about self-control. I find it difficult to suggest to the church member in need that maybe one of the reasons they have got themselves into such a pickle in the first place is their lack of self-control. When we look at the fruits of the Holy Spirit in Galatians 5:22–23, we rarely promote self-control as one of the attributes or signs of the Holy Spirit at work in someone's life. As followers of Jesus, determined disciples, and those wanting to be brave in our everyday world, self-control is an essential part of our development.

James wrote about the fruit produced being aligned with the seeds that we sow. If we want to bear the fruit of self-control in the future, then we begin by planting small steps of discipline today. Being a person of self-control is simple; it's just not easy. TV's Miranda Hart suggests, as she ponders writing a new diet book, that losing weight is simple: you just "eat less and wiggle about a bit more". But we know, either first hand or from friends who have struggled to lose weight, that it is far from easy. A friend recently heard someone say in a clothing shop while they were admiring the impressive window display, "I love those clothes but I love chocolate more." Self-control is another mirror that shows what is important to us. We all have the same twenty-four hours in a day, and we all make choices as to how we use them.

Self-control is not just about self-help or self-management; it is about submission as a disciple of Jesus Christ. It is saying, "I am unable to do this in my strength. I need the Holy Spirit to work within me and so I bring all my poor habits and addictions under the Lordship of Jesus Christ."

Every disciple comes under a rabbi or a teacher, and the more time we spend with them, the more we reflect the one we choose to follow. As we submit all the challenges we face each day, the decisions we make, the relationships we are investing in, the work that we do, the family that we are responsible for, we allow Him to take the reins. The bit goes into our mouth, the tiller, is taken out of our hands; the spark with forest fire potential is handed over, and the self-control looks more like returning ultimate control to our creator.

Step one of seeing new fruit in our determined discipleship is handing our lives once again to Jesus and saying, "We cannot tame it without you". Maybe the phrase "you can't teach an old dog new tricks" comes to mind as you are reading this. Well, the good news is that it may be a well-known proverb, but it is not a biblical proverb. The Bible promises in 2 Corinthians 5:17 that "if anyone is in Christ, the new creation has come: the old has gone, the new is here!" There are no old dogs in the kingdom of God; just fresh-faced new followers of Christ, and anything is possible if we are willing to let go and let God take control. Back in James 3:8 it states that "no human being can tame the tongue", but our hope is in God and His purposes, not in our own abilities.

The Power of Words

The childhood rhyme that "sticks and stones may break my bones but words will never hurt me" is simply not true. Often the words spoken to us, especially when we are children, are extremely powerful. Many adults, when we ask them about significant experiences from their childhood, will talk about a moment when a parent, sibling, friend, or teacher said a short phrase to them or about them which has stuck to them and haunted them for years, like some repeating mantra. Proverbs 18:21 reminds us that "the tongue has the power of life and death". It was through the words of God Himself in Genesis 1 that the world in all its beauty and magnificence was created.

Words are powerful.

Therefore, James starts this chapter by suggesting that "not many of you should become teachers" as teachers will be judged with greater degree of strictness. A school teacher has a classroom of children listening to their every word and watching their every action. School teachers in our society are given great trust, but one small error (verse 2), which reveals their true self for a moment, can be extremely damaging. A preacher on a Sunday at church has the power to exhort and encourage or to lay guilt and heaviness on those listening. A counsellor can use their words to speak life into a person at a very vulnerable moment of their life, or with a hasty comment do greater damage to an already challenging situation.

This is why, when people ask me about whether they should become involved in full-time Christian ministry, I always encourage them to consider carefully the responsibilities of ministering to others. It is not something to be taken up lightly, as much will be required of them.

The words of the reckless pierce like swords,
but the tongue of the wise brings healing.

Proverbs 12:18

It's not just *our* tongues that require control; it is also relevant to those around us. Gossip only does harm when it is shared. If you hear some juicy information about a friend or colleague, you may not always be able to stop the source of information but you can decide to not pass it on any further. Gossip is often a poorly timed comment overheard by an unwise person that is then passed on and shared by other people. A forest fire is started by one spark, but it requires the resources of the dense population of trees in the vicinity, or the tongues of others, to keep it alight.

As a firefighter for ten years with West Sussex Fire and Rescue, I know that a forest fire is physically one of the hardest of all fires to tackle. They often happen at the hottest time of the year and in places where there is limited access to water. The only way to put out such a fire is with long handled "beaters". These crude devices are large sections of thick leather attached to one end of a broom handle. As a fire crew, we would then slap the seats of fire all around until it was out. This would take many hours and would leave us physically exhausted. If the fire was too big and out of hand we would create a fire break. Based on the direction of the wind, we would move ahead of the fire and remove all possible fuel, such as trees and bushes, that would allow the fire to spread. This, too, was hard work.

As a hearer of gossip, we have the choice whether to pour petrol on the fire or to create a fire break. When gossip gets out of hand, it is hard work to put out and fully extinguish. Rumours can affect people for years after the incident first took place.

Proverbs 4:23 instructs us to guard our hearts. I am not who others say I am, or even who I think I am. I am who God says I am. Sometimes I am amazed by who or what I allow myself to listen to. Comments on social media by people who don't know me are not a true mirror of who I am. Sometimes, to guard my own heart I literally have to speak to myself in the mirror, reminding myself of the truths of what God says about me. I might meet with a friend, family member, or a church leader who has that, often undervalued, gift of the Holy Spirit, the gift of encouragement. The right people point me back to God and what He says about me, not what others may have assumed.

Gracious words are a honeycomb,
sweet to the soul and healing to the bones.

Proverbs 16:24

It is not helpful to constantly compare ourselves to others. Remember, comparison is the thief of all joy and steals all the potential that each one of us carries. Throwaway comments, both offline and online, sometimes meant in humour, can hurt people, and over time, if not dealt with properly, have a devastating effect.

At the tail end of 2009 my brother-in-law, Rich Hubbard, one of my best friends, was diagnosed with an aggressive cancer. We had thought something was wrong back in the summer but we couldn't see anything obvious in his appearance. There was some weight loss but we assumed that was because he had been dieting, but as his family we just felt something was just not right. Rich travelled a lot with his work as the CEO of Links International, an overseas charity working in many developing countries, and we wondered whether he had picked up a virus. In the early autumn, I took him to the Hospital for Tropical Diseases in London, where they ran countless tests. It soon became apparent that this was not a simple illness that could be cured with a couple of pills. This cruel and unseen disease was killing him from the inside, until he couldn't fight it any more, and we lost him in 2010. We were devastated.

Many of us will have experienced loss, and understand that moment when every part of us goes numb and nothing seems real. Grief hits us like an unexpected, pounding wave. In all the years since losing Rich, my thoughts have often been, "I wish I had known what was happening earlier. Maybe he could have had an operation and would still be with us." But we didn't know, because we couldn't see.

James reminds us about this in verse 14. If we harbour bitter envy and selfish ambition, this will eat away at us. It is a hidden illness. It is earthly, unspiritual, and demonic. Our words can be a hidden spiritual illness dressed up as criticism, but really it is deep-rooted cynicism, looking for the worst in someone else to make ourselves feel better. Dealing with the root of such illness is essential, before it begins to damage our lives, relationships, and church communities.

Out of the Same Mouth

Of course, we must use our tongue for various everyday activities. We may need it to discipline our children, talk with our peers, say loving things to our husband or wife, give instructions at work to our colleagues, sing songs of worship, pray to our Father God, communicate with the supermarket assistant, or even speak to Alexa on the Echo Dot. The challenge is for our words to be consistent. When we have a bad day at work and are cut up by another car on the drive home, we might react differently to the same scenario than we would at the end of a more positive day. We might be polite to the first cold call on our home telephone, but after the third time of being disturbed during the family evening meal, many of us, in frustration, will say something we regret.

My parents would often encourage my siblings and me that Philippians 4:8 is a useful guide for responding to one another. Only speak if it is true, noble, right, pure, lovely, admirable, excellent, or praiseworthy. Often, as children, we would say unkind things to one another, and then attempt to justify our actions and endeavour to persuade my parents that it was true or deserved.

We all can learn to listen more. More helpfully, we can practise speaking less and spending more time listening to others – really listening. This is a skill I am still learning. If you want people to listen to your thoughts, ideas, and stories, then start by listening to other people and showing interest in what they are passionate about. Everyone we meet has an incredible story if we are willing to ask the right questions and listen well. It is easy to get into negative conversations which moan about the boss, the lack of time we have, the weather we are experiencing. A better conversation is always one that builds others up by asking helpful questions and encouraging the other person in what they are passionate about. It is always better to light a candle than to curse the darkness, or, as the Roman politician and lawyer Marcus Tullius Cicero is alleged to have said, "Don't criticize, create something new."

Wise Words

Have you ever kept a log of what you are listening to? Asked the question, what words am I allowing access into my thoughts? What songs, TV shows, books, friendly advice, podcasts, internet sites are you allowing to shape your thinking? James in his writing suggested that all these things are earthly wisdom. What time are we spending listening to wisdom that comes from above? How much time do we spend in prayer, listening to our Father God, and meditating on His Word?

> Blessed is the one...
> whose delight is in the law of the Lord,
> and who meditates on his law day and night.
> That person is like a tree planted by streams of water
> ...whatever they do prospers.
>
> **Psalm 1:1–3**

When well-meaning Christians endeavour to provide their version of wisdom to correct people on what is deemed inappropriate behaviour or poor habits, we can come across as religious zealots or out-of-touch moaners. Our role as Christ followers is to come alongside one another, like the university accountability group that a youthful Krish benefited from; or, when gentle correction is required, we do it in love, using the Word of God, as Cris will be looking at in chapter five. James makes it clear that our efforts will always be second rate, so he encourages us to point to God, not our well-intentioned words or actions. Our mouths sing praises to God on one day and speak curses the next. We will always be seen by others as hypocritical, as we are human, and being human is to err.

We are a poor imitation of the real thing, but as determined disciples our desire is to become more like Him, to learn to live and love like Jesus did. Our well-meaning desire to help others needs to start by pointing to the source of wisdom: God Himself.

Creating a Healthy Culture

Do we know what our culture looks like? How do we know if it is healthy and giving life and strength to those around us?

James helpfully lists for us in verses 16 and 17 two different cultures and a way in which we can assess our present circumstances, whether it be in our marriage, family, workplace, or church.

Strong words in James 3:16 make it clear that if we look within ourselves and are struggling with jealousy and contention, then we have a culture of unruly behaviour and therefore every kind of evil practice. But if we are filled with godly wisdom (verse 17), then we will be "pure; then peace-loving, considerate, submissive, full of mercy and good fruit, impartial and sincere". That's a great character assessment I would love to have.

If we want to create healthy culture in our homes, workplaces, and churches, it needs to start with an assessment of the heart to be people filled with godly wisdom. That heart then overflows into words that uplift and encourage others, seeing the good in everyone and everything. We can choose to be "blessing only" people, whose tongue only speaks life; someone who gives thanks in all circumstances (1 Thessalonians 5:18) and chooses to always be joyful (1 Thessalonians 5:16). Or we can continue as a "blessing one moment, cursing the next" person.

This takes practice.

This requires determination. Determined disciples learn to tame the tongue so that they can be "blessing only" people!

A person finds joy in giving an apt reply –
and how good is a timely word!

Proverbs 15:23

- Learn to listen. Next time you meet someone, deliberatively engage in conversation and see if you can discover three new things about them before you tell them ONE thing about yourself. When it gets dark at night, light a candle and think about the times when you have brought light into dark places. Remember the moments when you have changed the conversation from one of gossip and criticism to one of encouragement and loving others. Pray for more opportunities for your words to bring life.

- What are we sowing? If we desire to reap good fruit with our lives, then we need to start by sowing good seeds. Write a list of all the people who have encouraged you or invested in your life in some way, and then send them a handwritten card by post. We all love receiving handwritten notes more than computer-printed junk mail.

Only the Brave

As has been mentioned in previous chapters, historical authors have written challenging commentaries about the book of James,[36] claiming that it doesn't portray the grace-centric gospel of Jesus very well and suggesting that it might encourage people back to a doctrine of works.

Some aspects of James can seem like a self-help book, but the writer also regularly points to God as the source of our help. He places the responsibility on each one of us as a follower of the way to bring about change, but by setting the bar so high, he also underlines the fact that we can never achieve it in our own strength.

The writer of James encourages us, as determined disciples, to tame our tongues, to think before we speak – not just on some occasions, but to train our tongues to consistently speak only love and praise. There is a great cost to this challenge, but also great reward. If we can get our tongue under control before unkind or unhelpful words tumble out, then we can get our mind, body, spirit, and all our earthly selves under control. In taming one small but powerful part of us, our whole person is affected. Unfortunately, there is no quick three-step programme, titled with a helpful acronym that is going to make this happen overnight. It requires one step at a time, one day at a time, making small improvements that lead to the greater goal. That is discipleship.

It requires bravery, it requires determination to TAME IT.

Further reading

N.T. Wright, *Following Jesus: Biblical Reflections on Discipleship* (revised edition, Eerdmans, 2014)

Graham Cray, *Disciples and Citizens: A Vision for Distinctive Living* (IVP, 2007)

Rick Warren, *The Purpose-Driven Life* (Zondervan, 2004)

Dave Ferguson & Jon Ferguson, *Exponential: How You and Your Friends Can Start a Missional Church Movement* (Zondervan, 2010)

Tom Wright, *Early Christian Letters for Everyone* (Society for Promoting Christian Knowledge, 2011)

Peter Scazzero, *Emotionally, Spiritually Healthy* (Zondervan, 2017)

Dietrich Bonhoeffer, *The Cost of Discipleship* (Touchstone, 1995)

Joseph Gisbey, *Follow: Walking in the Dust of the Rabbi* (Darton, Longman & Todd, 2015)

Testimony from Dan, 18, Harrogate

When I was younger I could barely speak at all. Not many people could understand me. Speech therapists told my parents that I wouldn't be able to go to a mainstream school. I began to feel quite down about myself, inferior to my peers. The biggest negative labels we carry are often the ones we put on ourselves.

At Soul Survivor I experienced Jesus' love for me in such a tangible way. It told me a completely different story. He told me there was no need for fear or shame, which was much more beautiful than feeling like I wasn't good enough. I realized it's not about me but all about what Jesus has done. It's not about how well I perform, but that I am simply a child of God. It just changed everything. It helped me to be much more confident. Originally I was quite shy and didn't have many friends, but as I began to love myself more I began to approach others more often. If all that mattered was what Jesus thought of me, I worried less about what others thought of me.

I am clumsy. I often drop stuff and make a fool of myself, but it's alright. I now know I don't need to take these things to heart, and it actually enables me to share some joy with people. That I am able to stand up and speak to share my story is an amazing testimony to how faithful our God is.

My speech is still not perfect; I still pronounce some stuff slightly differently, but I realize that God makes beautiful things out of our weaknesses and they become our strengths. I spent ten minutes in hysterical laughter with a friend about the way I say "humour". Apparently it's humorous. God has turned something I was ashamed of into something that can bring joy.

I don't often feel brave. It's a real challenge to hold on to what God says about us and to keep our eyes on Him instead of ourselves.

I've got a really strange phobia of balloons. Obviously a balloon isn't going to hurt me – it's just a piece of synthetic rubber with a few innocent air molecules in it – but fear gets inflated! Once I was in a worship service and all these balloons came out – it was meant to be a celebration, but for me it felt like torment! The real challenge during that worship time was to focus on Jesus and forget the fear, to fix my eyes on Jesus! And I reckon if I did that more, I would step out a bit more for Him.

MEET CATHY MADAVAN: interview by Sim Dendy

What inspires you about where you live?

Mark and I have loved bringing up our two teenage daughters on the south coast of England where we have been part of Locks Heath Free Church for the past fourteen years. We love being so close to the sea, and we love wandering along the seafront or the River Hamble where we can watch people sailing or kite-surfing on the water. The scenery is always changing and the ocean reminds us how amazing our planet is.

Living so close to the sea, do you go sailing regularly?

Never! I fancy getting a kayak, though.

So, water aside, what would your perfect day look like?

Personally, I am partial to lying on the sofa with a fantastic book, accompanied by a large pot of coffee and a small pile of cakes, in silence. And by silence, I do mean complete silence. Ideally, no one else will even be breathing near me! Once I've had some "me time", however, nothing compares with spending time as a family, playing board games, chatting, watching TV together, or hanging out around the firepit with friends.

What is it about the book of James that excites you?

When my teenage daughters go out at night, one of the last things I cheekily say to them is, "Make wise choices!" Sometimes I wonder if we ought to say the same thing to each other before we leave church on a Sunday. Really, this is what James was doing as he wrote this letter – telling his readers to make good choices with their lives and to live out what they believe. It's not a subtle book, and I rather like that about it.

Where do you think we need to be particularly brave as disciples?

Sometimes the bravest thing we can do is to keep on keeping on. I think it takes real courage to just stay on the path and not give up. Most of us will go through seasons as disciples where we face huge challenges, and following Jesus and His commands can be tough. But we must raise the bar as disciples and cheer each other on as we honestly share our triumphs and our tragedies. We need each other so much. As we persevere together we discover a greater intimacy with Christ and His suffering, and also a deeper connection with each other as a result.

What one thing has really helped you in your discipleship?

The obvious answer to this is the amazing people who have invested in me and encouraged me over the years. But the other people who have helped in me in my Christian faith have been wonderful Christian writers and songwriters. I just don't know how people grow without reading or listening to audio books and music. I always seem to have about three books on the go. We all need to feed our soul and we are blessed with so many fantastic resources to choose from.

LOSE IT

CATHY MADAVAN

God opposes the proud but shows favour to the humble.
James 4:6

I *think it is fair to say that "losing it"* is not something we would normally aspire to. Certainly, if I were to say to my family that I am going to "lose it", that would not have positive connotations. They would understandably assume that either I was about to have a slight emotional eruption or that I was about to come last in a race or a board game (losing as usual), or maybe even that I was about to misplace something important by putting it somewhere that I thought I wouldn't forget but then would apparently lose it forever. Losing it is not usually perceived as a good thing.

So why on earth would anybody ever choose to lose?

Whatever our natural instincts of self-preservation and self-promotion might be, Jesus in Matthew 16:25 clearly tells us that "whoever wants to save their life will lose it, but whoever loses their life for me will find it". This sounds demanding (and perhaps it is), but it also sounds exciting and full of possibility. But what exactly does losing our life for Christ mean to those of us who are disciples of Jesus today? How do we, in the busyness and challenges of each day, engage in this divine exchange where we simultaneously lose and find life in the midst of it? And, let's be honest, what we *really* want to know is, how much bravery is it going to take to "lose it" – and is that cost just too high?

STRENGTH IN HUMILITY

Having previously considered how we need to Face It, Live It, and Tame It, chapter 4 of the book of James continues the themes of self-control and determined discipleship. But the writer presses us further. In these verses, the author has given us the best possible chance of unravelling the mystery and marvel of how we find life in its fullness as we lose our grip over it. Of course, whenever James writes about external behaviour, it is always inextricably linked to internal choices. Therefore, there are deep wells of wisdom in this chapter about straightening out our motives. This matters because whatever we see is always shaped by what we cannot see; what is public always begins with what is private, and everything we do is a consequence of who we are.

If we assume that the writer of James was, as most commentators agree, James the brother of Jesus, we can read these words with the knowledge that he would have witnessed Jesus from a unique perspective. Having watched Jesus grow up and having seen Him live and die, motivated by mercy, justice, and unconditional love, James wrote this epistle with clarity and authority on what pure motives really look like in action.

So how do we respond when we know our own motives are, frankly, mixed at best and our desires are often less than pure and humble? Thankfully we are not on our own, and the Holy Spirit will always lead us forward from where we are. As we dwell in the Lord's presence, as we spend time in His Word, and as we invest in authentic and accountable relationships, He will gently but firmly challenge us about the words we speak, the prejudice we show, or the murky motives that so easily take root in our souls. But make no mistake, the guidance in James is as clear to us as a bell and almost binary in approach – it is basically our way or God's way. That is the choice we face. It's as if James is reminding us that we can't ever truly say, "No, Lord." Either He is Lord of all or He is not Lord at all, as the saying goes.

Learning to "lose it" is understanding that it is the humble people who are, in fact, the strong ones. David Field, exploring this chapter of James, explains that "humility is the passport to strength".[37] He shows that James teaches that it is the proud, the self-sufficient, and those who always think they are right who display all the hallmarks of weakness. When we will not admit our mistakes or we try to work out faith with our own resources, we are not able to grasp the full extent of our salvation, nor can we receive empowerment from the Holy Spirit. Truly strong people, on the other hand, are those who know that every victory, large or small, is won as we take up our cross, put on our spiritual armour, and depend on Christ alone.

While the world around us desperately attempts to clamber up the ladder of status and significance, we must in contrast empty ourselves so that He can fill us. The American evangelist D. L. Moody, who was at the heart of a remarkable move of God in the 1800s, put it like this: "God sends no one away empty except those who are full of themselves." When we are brimming with too much of our own importance we simply fail to leave room for the Holy Spirit to do His work. Therefore, our petty squabbles and excursions into self-righteousness are, according to James, a direct result of us failing to lose control over our life. Like a mutinous crew on a ship, we constantly attempt to grab the wheel from the Captain of our soul, even though He is the only one who knows how to navigate us safely to our destination.

One thing is crystal clear, then, as we consider the words of chapter 4. James believes that surrendering every element of who we are to God is a pivotal part of what it means to bravely follow Jesus. In his characteristically forthright way, his words help us to grapple with both the spiritual significance of this truth and the practical implications of how to show self-discipline and surrender our lives daily.

HEAD: THE BATTLE OF SURRENDER

I have always been fascinated by genealogy. I have a copy of our family tree traced back a few hundred years which reveals extraordinary names like Cissy Inkpen and rather fascinating careers including a lion tamer. One member of our family insists he has traced our line back to Cleopatra, which would at least explain my thirty-year addiction to black eyeliner. This interest in history means I am always drawn to the coats of arms that are often displayed at the entrances of aristocratic homes. These distinguished plaques apparently originated in the twelfth century, when knights in battle, significant families, or those in civic roles were identified immediately by their heraldry. In many ways, the coat of arms behaved much like a modern-day logo would –

clearly identifying your allegiance and loyalty or signifying that you belonged to a certain family or tribe. In a feudal medieval society, your affiliations were of huge significance and might even be a matter of life or death. But while society has changed over the centuries, the question of who we align ourselves with remains a crucial one both in our identity and in our purpose.

We all have a deep-rooted need to be part of a community or tribe. We all need people who are our people, whether that is a family, church, community organization, friendship group, or school. Some people apparently bond with other people who own pugs. Each to their own. We all long to belong. While those places might be significant, being part of God's family is the ultimate answer to that longing. When we surrender our life to Christ and receive His salvation, that means we pledge our allegiance to our heavenly King *and* His chosen people. Loyalty and faithfulness are paramount principles for Jesus followers. So if the "royal law" (James 2:8) of faithfully loving God and loving our neighbour as ourself is at the core of our faith, James wants in this chapter to focus our attention again upon anything that could potentially disrupt that crucial unity with God and others. If we are loyal to Christ, then any opposition to our allegiance needs to be dealt with. It all boils down to the question of who is in charge of our life. Whose coat of arms are we displaying and how proudly do we display it? Bluntly put, this means asking ourselves whether our actions consistently match up to our declarations of who we follow. Can the people we know identify our allegiance to God by what they see and hear from us?

Although we might not be knights jousting on behalf of a king, James makes clear that we are indeed in a battle and we *are* called to clearly identify ourselves with the King of kings. In fact, the original language James uses in the first two verses of chapter 4 are fierce and arguably military in nature and have been translated variably into words such as fights, conflicts, battle, quarrel, kill, fight, wage war. This rather brutal language necessarily conveys the severity of what it means when we are at war with our own passions and desires or at war with others – which we often are because of those same selfish desires. Alec Motyer explains it well:

> *James chose the vocabulary of war to express controversies and quarrels, animosity and bad feeling among Christians, not because there is no other way of saying it, but because there is no other way of expressing the horror of it.*[38]

As we might become desensitized to the many images of war or famine we see on our television and computer screens, so we might also become blasé about the devastation that is caused when we fall out with others or turn away from God's best for our life. Week by week we witness another squabble, absorb another bit of gossip, or jettison prayer and Scripture reading from our priorities list. We habitually respond to challenges more from a place of our own desires and defensiveness rather than the determined discipleship that enables us to stand alongside others and stand firm for Christ. The sad thing is that our spiritual malaise doesn't always impact us as it should, let alone fill us with horror, and yet the consequences of our sometimes-flabby faith or our casual conflicts are far reaching.

Selfless Prayer

Even our prayer life (which would be the clear and obvious antidote to our selfish motives) can, if we are not careful, be corrupted by our own self-absorption (James 4:1–2). James highlights this and then goes straight for the jugular, naming envy specifically as a gateway for our fickle motives and our constant desire for more. It's true and we know it. But rather than stepping off the grinding treadmill of envy, which offers no real contentment or spiritual health, we keep pounding on, day after day, expending energy but going nowhere quickly. We keep stepping out into jealousy, wishing for what we don't have, striding toward success, significance, and all that glittering stuff that we imagine is over the horizon but which never delivers what it promises. And so our prayers become a reflection of this, often stuck in patterns of asking for more, rather than considering how we might honour and serve God with what we already have

I have lost count how many times over the years I have heard the words from verse 2, "You do not have because you do not ask God," quoted, often by those who suppose that God will pay out like a holy slot machine if we confess our requests to Him, whatever they might be. But surely we should pay equal attention to the verses around those words, which emphasize our unfaithfulness in contrast to God's unfailing love. God is asking us to realign our motives as we pray, as His are not ever in question.

Selfish desires are not a new phenomenon, of course. Adam set the ball rolling and it has never stopped since. Take almost any Bible narrative and before long the internal battle between what the person (or people) wants and what God wants is found at the heart of the story. David envied another man's wife and acted to get what he wanted, with tragic results (2 Samuel 11), Saul envied David's talent and leadership and it led to misery for all concerned (1 Samuel 18). Moving to the New Testament, I wonder if Ananias and Sapphira envied the attention and accolades others received as they gave publicly but also desired their possessions for themselves, leading to their demise (Acts 5:1–11). Even the disciples coveted influence and position as they jostled and argued over who would be the greatest (Luke 9:46–48).

Human nature grasps for power, for position, and for possessions, and none of us is immune, especially in a culture where consumerism is described by experts as the amniotic fluid in which we live and breathe.[39] Make no mistake, consumerism has taken a firm root in our culture. As I spoke to many church leaders this year in preparation for the writing of this chapter, the consumer mindset was cited repeatedly as one of the major forces impacting the church in the UK. One church leader in Peterborough described a continual cultural shift from a "battleship mentality", where everybody has a role, a goal, and clear trust in the leaders, toward a "cruise ship mentality", where a small minority work hard so that the majority turn up, receive, and criticize where the ship is heading and how they are being served. That kind of insight should make us all stop and think. Are we really becoming people who treat church or faith simply as something to meet our needs as part of our quest to have a comfortable life that suits us perfectly? Are we so afraid of commitment that we fail to appreciate the potential wrapped up in the body of Christ if we all play our part?

Of course, most of us do not intend to be like this, but our desires are always busy finding new things to want, and we often feed those desires like hungry children. I am guessing we have all been there: we don't think we need a new car until we visit our friends and sit in their snazzy new vehicle and hear them waxing lyrical about their hybrid engine and Bluetooth technology. Suddenly, not only would we now *like* a new car, but we persuade ourselves we absolutely *need* one. Or maybe we don't think we want to sing a solo or take a leadership position until *that* person who has being doing it *far* less time than we have is asked to do it, and then we feel total indignation at being overlooked. And those of us who are parents know we are oh so relaxed about the speed our child potty trains or speaks until we go to the toddler group and hear how heroic Harriet has mastered it all in a few days. Suddenly we find ourselves throwing away the nappies and repeating key phrases over and over. It's all a bit ridiculous, really. The reluctant truth is that we probably all tend to look at others who have certain positions, friendships, lifestyles, or (if we are going to be painfully honest) even ministries, and if we are not fully surrendered to God and content to fly His banner alone, our heart so easily becomes polluted and our relationships tangled.

C. S. Lewis hit the nail on the head when, in his book *Mere Christianity*, he said, "If I find in myself desires which nothing in this world can satisfy, the only logical explanation is that I was made for another world."[40] We were never intended to be fulfilled by the treasures of this world, and yet that is so often what we settle for.

So, in chapter 4, James' words provoke us to loosen our grip on the things that distract us and to keep the main thing the main thing – to fix our eyes on God. As we pray and ask for wisdom and help, the fundamental question we are being prompted to continually ask is whether we are loyal to the One from whom we ask these things (verses 1–3). Have we settled for praying about all we are wishing for instead of daily surrendering our hearts to the One who fulfils our every need? Are we committed to His purposes and plans above all else? This is challenging stuff. As we hold up the mirror again we might consider conducting a personal spiritual audit to discern whether it is predominantly our own personal satisfaction that motivates us in our prayers or whether we are prepared to loosen our grip over our own desires to make room for the life in all its fullness that Jesus has in mind for us. This isn't because God wants to make life hard or punish us – quite the reverse. It is because He has more for us than our minds can sometimes fathom, and it is as we know His mind above ours that we discover the adventure of faith in all its splendour.

This repositioning of ourselves is all part of the upside down, inside out kingdom of God, where the last shall be first and death brings life. As Christians, the way down is always the way up: "Humble yourselves before the Lord, and he will lift you up" (James 4:10). It is as we lose something less significant that we will win something far greater. Even Jesus, when facing His own battle in the Garden of Gethsemane, had to *choose* to go His Father's way as He said, "Not my will, but yours be done" (Luke 22:42), despite the almost unbearable cost. As He chose to relinquish that control, He reversed the decision Adam made to grasp it, and reinstated the possibility of us living in relationship with a Holy God once again. Jesus' prayer and actions were the ultimate act of humility and the perfect picture of faith and works as one. Philippians 2:5–7 reminds us that, "Jesus… though he was in the form of God, did not count

equality with God a thing to be grasped, but made himself nothing"
(ESV). Jesus lived to do His Father's business. That was where His
loyalty lay, and He lived out that decision every day in His heart,
mind, and actions, even if that meant losing His life.

We too are called to die to self; to place Jesus and His
instructions above all else; to go as the Holy Spirit leads us. In many
ways, we are being called to die a thousand little deaths each day as
we prioritize His ways over ours in our relationships, our finances,
and our habits, thereby discovering a thousand blessings along
the way. These choices lead us to discover that the narrow path of
determined discipleship always leads to the wide-open spaces of
grace. What could possibly substitute for knowing God's presence,
peace, and purpose after all?

Powerful Choices

So much of our walk with Jesus, indeed our life, comes down to
making these daily choices. Sometimes we simply buy into the
false premise that we are not able to change a situation or have no
options. We believe we are stuck and therefore we become stuck.
But this is a lie. We may not always be able to determine our
circumstances, but we definitely have a say over how we respond
to those circumstances, and those decisions are powerful. You and
I can choose what we will say, do, forgive, love, invest in, and pray
about. We can choose the company we keep; we can choose what
we hold on to and what we release. We can choose whether to make
a situation better or worse, to build up or to tear down. When we
feel overwhelmed with the scale of all that needs to be done or the
state of the world, we have a choice about our response: either we
retreat into whatever our default comfort setting may be, sticking
our head into the sand or a series on Netflix, or we choose to do
something, to say something, to pray something instead. We can
choose to believe the lie that we can't make any difference, or we can
press in and press on and follow Jesus through our circumstances,
knowing He is with us and is above all things.

And, lest we forget, faithful Christians around the globe have unimaginable choices to make. Many still do lay down their lives for their faith, still choose to declare their allegiance to Christ with crosses proudly displayed in their windows in the full knowledge of what that might mean for them and their loved ones. For these persecuted brothers and sisters, the words of Paul, "to live is Christ and to die is gain" (Philippians 1:21), are more than a philosophical sentiment or a well-crafted line from a song. It is a reality they may well have to face. Other believers bravely choose to keep worshipping and keep trusting when on the face of it their poverty and lack of material provision would test us all. They still believe that God is good, they still give and care and pray even when life is far from good.

From time to time I think back to occasions when I have experienced the hospitality of people who have had so little to share. I remember sharing a sunset feast with Syrian refugees in a camp who pooled their resources and created seating out of scavenged items so that we would be comfortable and welcome. I recall the outrageous generosity of a woman in Africa, who shared one of her very few precious mangos from her tree with me as we sat and sang on the floor of her shelter. As I remember these precious moments, I am reminded that we all have choices about how we live, how we love others, and what we trust in, and I am challenged to be braver with all that God has given to me.

James asks us all to settle the matter in our minds and to deliberately lose the battle over who is in charge of our life – to surrender fully to Christ. It might not always be easy or comfortable; it could mean investing our time and resources differently or making decisions with a countercultural set of values, but it is there we find the greatest freedom. More than ever, the next generation of believers needs a church that has decided where its allegiance lies. If we decide to dilute our faith, and we model a wishy-washy version of the truth that, in reality, looks more like the self-absorbed and divided world around us, it will be hard for them (never mind others) to distinguish what the genuine article really looks like.

It is a brave and bold decision to surrender to God, but His arms are also the safest and most secure place we will ever find. Without a doubt, declaring allegiance to Christ is the best and most liberating decision we could ever make. The book of James is simply asking us to wave our banner with pride and to declare, by the Spirit, that we are on the Lord's side.

WHAT STOPS US FROM GIVING THE REINS OF OUR LIVES BACK TO GOD (LOSING IT!)?

James highlights the selfish desires inside us all. Which of these are particular issues for you as you seek to be a determined disciple?

- ❏ Self-gratification
- ❏ Self-fulfilment
- ❏ Self-determination
- ❏ Self-pity
- ❏ Self-esteem issues
- ❏ Self-indulgence
- ❏ Self-interest
- ❏ Self-sufficiency
- ❏ Self-deception
- ❏ Self-promotion
- ❏ Self-righteousness

What helps us to give the reins back to God?

Thinking of the areas above where you most struggle to relinquish control, how would the following help you to surrender more fully to Christ?

❏ Self-discipline (holy habits and perseverance which lead to a way of life)

❏ Self-assessment (having a sober and accurate judgment of myself)

❏ Self-awareness (knowing when I am doing it wrong or right!)

❏ Self-acceptance (knowing I am not a mistake and fearfully and wonderfully made)

❏ Self-esteem (knowing my identity and confidence is in Christ not me)

❏ Self-restraint (walking away or biting the tongue)

❏ Self-control (avoiding excess or temptation)

❏ Self-starting (trusting that God has given resources to do what He asks me to do – and doing it)

❏ Self-sacrifice (actively caring about the needs of others)

❏ Self-respect (knowing I am worth caring about and that I matter)

Reflect on your answers. Perhaps you could journal, pray, or talk with a trusted friend about surrendering your life more fully to God and His truth. What powerful choice could you make today that would draw you closer to Christ?

HEART: FORSAKING ALL OTHERS

It seems impossible but it is true: twenty-five years ago (when I was young – *really* young) I walked down the aisle to marry Mark. We didn't have much of a clue about what marriage would entail and, unsurprisingly, there have been some memorable mountains and a few dark valleys along the way. He is, though, I think, beginning to get used to me now – or perhaps he has just learned to smile and nod in the appropriate places. In any case, that commitment has been a firm foundation for which I am truly grateful.

The year before our wedding, however, I made another sacred vow: I decided to turn my back on my past and to wholeheartedly follow Jesus wherever He would lead me. It was an intensely personal and intimate decision, and it changed my life forever. The good news of Jesus really does have the power to totally transform lives, and so we, His disciples, are called to confidently go and make more disciples (Matthew 28:16–20).

Whether your own conversion was a specific moment or more a series of moments, the prayers you uttered as you promised to be faithful and loyal to Christ all the days of your life were indeed sacred vows. We are each part of this beautiful covenant relationship of commitment and love. We do not make these promises because we have been coerced or cajoled into it but because we love God and because He loved us first; He lavished His mercy and forgiveness upon us when we least deserved it. We give ourselves up willingly because He gave Himself for us, and we persevere in our faith because He never gives up on us. Whoever we are, and whatever we have had to overcome, our Saviour and King is also the lover of our soul, and He is jealous for our affection (James 4:5).

But this wonderful and personal faith is not supposed to be a solitary or individual pursuit. We were never supposed to be isolated Christians working out our relationship with God (or any other relationship) on our own. James was writing his letter to the believers together and reminds them as a community of their need to stay faithful (James 4:4-5). We are, the Bible says, *together* the bride of Christ (see, for example, Revelation 19:7–9), waiting for our bridegroom, and *together* we are called to prepare ourselves for the One we love. We need each other if we are both to stay the course and to grow as determined disciples more like the One we love and serve.

I am always grateful for the artists, designers, and filmmakers who express ideas and concepts in ways I never could with words alone. So often, through their gifts, we are freed to imagine and discover new depths and dimensions to what we had previously understood. Years ago, a friend of mine, Anita Collier – a talented artist with a clear prophetic gift – painted a particularly beautiful picture of a bride. Of course, the bride is radiant, as you would expect. Her dress is almost an iridescent white and she is, upon first glance at least, ready and prepared to meet her bridegroom. But then the artist invites us to look past the obvious and to imagine the bride somewhere unexpected, to complete the picture in our minds. We are therefore drawn away from her beauty to visualize the setting around her more fully. We are asked to imagine her standing at a bar in a pub, and a shabby one at that. It is dark, gloomy, and, in my mind's eye at least, overwhelmingly brown. We can almost mentally touch the sticky residue of beer on the wooden bar where the bride rests her hand, and feel the tackiness of the carpet underfoot; the heavy smell of hops and tobacco are contaminating the air. It's certainly not the sort of place one would expect a bride to be lingering in her exquisite gown. So, looking for clues, we turn back to the bride, observing her face for an insight as to why she would be there, and we suddenly realize that her expression, which at first seemed coy, is actually slightly seductive. She is looking over her shoulder and teasing us. She is a bride, but she is far from pure. She might look the part, but her loyalty is divided and her faithfulness is far from guaranteed.

The artist called this partially painted, partially imagined image, *Flirting with the World*, and invited us to consider our own feelings about that picture and what that setting (or indeed an alternative backdrop) might represent to us.

I remember engaging deeply with this bride picture, responding with a range of initial emotions: betrayal for sure, disappointment that the beautiful image had been tainted by something sinister, and conversely guilt as I considered my own personal fragility. But then I mentally stepped back and began to feel heartbroken and convicted at how God must see His beautiful bride that is His church – so often looking the part but toying with temptation; wearing the right clothes on a Sunday but winking at the values of the world on Monday; individually and corporately so often making choices that are incongruent with the faith we outwardly profess.

James' visual choice of language is equally hard to take in. He writes rather starkly in verse 4 that the church are adulterous people, enjoying a relationship with the world that means enmity against God. Faithfulness is a critical issue. We can't live peacefully in our union with God or each other while we are also trying to be best friends with the world, hanging out with her attitudes and flirting with her values. It's worth noticing that it is not brazen behaviour that James refers to as being so dangerous; it is simply the constant clamour of a culture that promotes self-indulgence and self-gratification, polluting hearts and minds and leading followers away from their covenant relationships.

This letter has plenty to say to us today. Unrestrained opinions, desires, words, and actions are still packed with the potential to undermine our precious unity with each other and with God. Faithfulness matters, and self-discipline is that faithfulness in action.

A Passion for Purity

Over the last twenty years or so that my husband has been in ministry in the Baptist Church, we have both had the privilege, and sometimes the trauma, of being invited behind the scenes of people's lives. Perhaps the greatest challenge of these two decades has been walking with precious people who come to church week after week, who might have five versions of the Bible on their bookshelves and another three on their phones, who have prayer groups, friendship groups, and sometimes a Christian heritage others would envy, and yet who make small incremental choices or sudden catastrophic decisions that cause a long-term slide into despondency and bitterness, or, in the worst cases, the destruction of the very things they love the most. As Mark and I have been invited into the secret places of people's lives, in all the messy brokenness and accompanying humility that often come with confession, we have witnessed and grieved over the implications and consequences of flirting with the world. Whether that compromise looks like foolish or selfish financial decisions, misplaced ambition, falling into the arms of somebody who was not a spouse, or an untempered desire to control others but not themselves, there are myriad examples of the selfish desire that James challenges us about in this chapter. The results, however, are consistently heartbreaking.

And of course, as I reflect on these interactions with others, I am painfully aware of the dark secrets of my own soul and the many times I have dived into the murky pool of selfishness and consequently disappointed myself, others, and ultimately God. The truth is, as a ministry BOGOF (Buy One Get One Free), I was not adequately prepared for the reality of life in Christian leadership when we set out with energetic youthful idealism combined with my own articulated lorry-load of baggage to sort out in a public role. It is a peculiar thing being a pastor's wife. I have no official position or area of clear authority in our church, but I am aware (having learned the hard way) that I carry great influence and that what I say or do not say is more significant than I am always comfortable with. I have also come to realize that living in a goldfish bowl as a family, where folk can observe you swimming through life (often in circles with your mouth open, unsure of where to go next), is challenging when you are very aware of your own visible and invisible shortcomings.

As you know, leaders are not invincible. I will confess that I too have felt the pressure to wear the frock, look the part, and play the role, when my own heart was dallying with the devil, feeding my own desires, and justifying my own behaviour. I have spoken at events about family life while wrestling with pressures in my own marriage or parenting. I have isolated myself from the wisdom of others when I haven't wanted to face the truth about my own flaws. And I'm not going to pretend that this is all in the past tense and that I am now always a paragon of virtue.

Nobody is perfect, and any expectation of perfection from ministry couples – or indeed from *any* person – is unreasonable and unhelpful. After all, we have all sinned and fallen short of the glory of God (Romans 3:23). But that doesn't mean we just wallow about and accept that we are probably all doomed to be unfaithful failures. Christ died for us so that we might know life in all its fullness (John 10:10). As we pray and cultivate a sensitivity to the Holy Spirit, read Scripture, and live in deep, authentic relationships, He will help us to reject perfectionism but embrace a persistent passion for purity. We are called to be followers who care deeply about holy living, and we also need friends and leaders who will lovingly help us to get back on track from time to time. This correction is not so that we live in condemnation but so that we can know forgiveness and restoration and grow in Christlikeness. That is God's goal for us. We can wave God's banner for all we are worth, but we also have the capacity to flirt with the world in a way that taints our relationship with God and others. It takes a determined disciple to pursue the right thing.

The Gift of Grace

The good news is that Pastor James, who was the leader of the Jerusalem church, does not leave us in this chapter feeling hopeless and helpless, sinking as we consider our endless list of shortcomings. He knows that the gospel is good news and he shifts gears mid-chapter to remind us that God is *longing* for us to be in relationship with him and therefore always "gives us more grace" (verses 5–6).

Thank God that there is always more grace. Where shame says that we are unacceptable, grace says we are not only acceptable but also loved. God's grace is immeasurable and inexhaustible and we certainly do not deserve it, but He extends it to us anyway because He loves us unconditionally. God never holds back on His children. He lavishes His love on us in a way we could never earn for ourselves. That does not, of course, mean that we should take His grace for granted, treating it as a cheap sticking plaster to cover our self-inflicted scrapes as we throw ourselves into the fire again knowing He will be there to sort us out (Romans 6:1–2). The extent of God's grace should lead us toward the grace-giver, not away from Him.

Grace, as we already know, is one of the grand themes of Scripture. Krish helpfully unpacked the apparent tension between "grace" and "works" in chapter two, reminding us that we are saved by grace alone for good works. John 1:14 tells us that Jesus, who embodied the love of God, was described as "full of grace". He was so full that He overflowed this unmerited favour and blessing to us, His disciples.

We also learn that:

- **We are called by grace (Galatians 1:15)**
- **We are saved by grace (Ephesians 2:1–9)**
- **We are given eternal life by grace (Romans 5:21)**

There is not a part of your life that has not been touched by this grace. From before you were born, to the condition of your soul, to your eternal destiny, everything is touched by God's unconditional love for you. You have been given hope and secured an eternal home. Every mistake you have made and every challenge you face is massively outweighed by His forgiveness and strength. There is *always* more grace. How can we not be overwhelmed by His glorious provision? Surely our only reasonable response is to receive His glorious gifts with a grateful heart, full of worship.

For some of us, however, receiving a gift is not so easy. We would prefer to be the one offering help, giving the compliment, or dispensing grace to others rather than being on the receiving end. Either because of pride, learned independence, or insecurity, we find it hard to receive from people. But that tendency begs the question whether it is also hard for us to receive from God. Just as we must learn to open our hands and hearts to others, so we need to be willing to allow God to pour out all He has for us. By automatically assuming the posture of one who always copes on our own, we deny Him (and others) the opportunity of freely giving with a generous heart.

I clearly remember when I realized I needed to learn to receive the grace of God in a new way. I had been working too hard (a recurring theme in my life), speaking and writing and doing things for God, but in an entirely unsustainable way. Whatever my mixed motives were, I found myself propelled forward on a treacherous path of relentless activity that I had paved for myself.

One night, as I slept in a hotel room after a day at another conference, the grace of God rather literally broke into my room. In the early hours of the morning I became aware of something near me. I woke suddenly and sat up, realizing that the lights were on and there was a man standing at the end of my bed. As you would expect, I immediately let out a blood-curdling scream and the man froze as we both became more fully cognisant of this less-than-ideal situation. He, it turned out, had been given my room key by the receptionist whose computer had not registered that the room already had an occupant. Excellent. So, bewildered and with his ears ringing, he stumbled back out and I, still half asleep and mildly traumatized, called the receptionist to thoroughly bless her down the phone – or something like that. When morning came, I descended, bleary-eyed, down to the reception where I was met by the hotel manager, who apologized profusely and asked me, "What is it that I can do for you?" Being British, I mumbled something incomprehensible about not worrying, thanking him for noticing, and reassuring him not to worry, or some such nonsense. But this manager would not hear of it. He not only refunded my visit but also lavished me with treats, cocktails in the bar, snacks, and the excessive attention that would be awarded to a visiting VIP.

As I dealt with the discomfort of this disproportionate (as I saw it) response, I suddenly realized that the manager had asked me the same question that Jesus had asked Bartimaeus when He met him: "What is it that I can do for you?" (Mark 10:51). And just as Bartimaeus received more healing, forgiveness, and hope than he could ever have dreamed of, so I realized how much love and grace God had poured into my life. Disproportionate grace. Extravagant grace. Outrageous and undeserved grace that had turned my life around. Forgiveness that I could never earn no matter how hard I worked. But instead of receiving this blessing and following Jesus with renewed commitment as Bartimaeus did, I had often settled for the same standard, rather awkward response, mumbling thanks for being noticed but assuming God must have better things to do than to worry about me. I had never really lived in or enjoyed the freedom that grace offers. I had never fully accepted or received His unconditional love for me. I can only tell you that as the Spirit spoke to me, something broke that needed to break in me, and I was more open and determined than ever to fully receive and live in that glorious grace. Perhaps this might not sound brave or like a big act of surrender to most people, but to a person as independent, defensive, and self-sufficient as I have been (albeit for some understandable reasons), it was a game changer. I can honestly say that I have been different after that experience. I double lock my hotel room doors for a start.

We were never made to just get through, coping on our own. Jesus' death on the cross and His magnificent resurrection were not supposed to accomplish just enough to keep our grace tank from drying out so we can tick along, bumping at the bottom of our resources, coping on the dregs of His goodness. His sacrifice is worth so much more than that. The Spirit was given to us so that we do not have to live within our own finite natural reserves. Galatians 5:1 tells us, "It is for freedom that Christ has set us free." Yes, this grace is gratuitously disproportionate and can even be overwhelming, but we should not bat it away because we do not feel worthy of it. We are filled with the Spirit so that our lives are receptacles and conduits of His abundant grace. There *is* always more grace, and that grace is the fuel for Christ-centred living. We are not brave or determined because we ourselves have all the resources in the world, but because He does and He is with us.

YES BUT HOW?

- How are you most likely to be seduced by the culture around you? Where do you flirt with the world or even dance with the enemy? Come to God in prayer about these areas.

- How do you think God feels when His people are unfaithful? What stops people from stepping out of a covenant relationship? How can we remain loyal?

- Can you identify the hallmarks of consumerism that have infiltrated the church and your own faith? How do we manage to surrender it all in a culture that tells us to gain it all?

- Take time to imagine that picture of the bride. What do you think God would want to say to His church in your area? To His church as a whole?

- How easy or hard do you find it to receive gifts or help from others? How easy or hard do you find it to receive from God?

- Look again at the words of the hymn "Amazing Grace". How amazed are you at God's lavish love for you?

- Learn to be still. Start with five minutes every day. After one week, add another five minutes. Use this time waiting for God. Don't pray to Him; wait for Him. Don't work on that to-do list. Don't plan what you're cooking for dinner. Just be still. Be quiet and wait. It's not easy at first, but it gets easier.

Give Your Burdens to God

Think of the concerns, mistakes, challenges, or issues that are currently weighing you down. Find some heavy items – pebbles, jars or cans of food, or books, for example. For each of the burdens on your mind, place an item into a bag to hold. Feel the weight of them. When you are ready, place your weight down and read Matthew 11:28–30:

> *"Come to me, all you who are weary and burdened, and I will give you rest. Take my yoke upon you and learn from me, for I am gentle and humble in heart, and you will find rest for your souls. For my yoke is easy and my burden is light."*

Thank God that His grace outweighs these things you are carrying. Give Him the things on your mind and receive His forgiveness, His peace, and His rest.

HANDS: LIVING IN HUMBLE SUBMISSION

James, as the church leader in Jerusalem, was at heart a practical pastor writing to a scattered church against a backdrop of an increasingly turbulent Roman Judea. He knew that following faithfully would require all kinds of wisdom and determination. At times, his letter reads almost like the Old Testament book of Proverbs in a New Testament context, encouraging his flock in memorable short axioms to do good, to care for the oppressed, to stay holy, and to live according to the wisdom of heaven. James did not introduce reams of new theological insights in this punchy letter or delve into the intricacies of interpreting Scripture; he was primarily concerned with encouraging those young Christians to put into practice the wisdom they already knew, and he exhorted them (and therefore us) to be consistent, to persevere, and to remain united whatever the challenges.

Pushing further forward into chapter 4 and dipping into chapter 5, we read some incredibly practical instructions from James to help believers stay on track as we seek to live as wholehearted and determined disciples. After all, surrender to God is not simply about relinquishing control and hoping for the best. The epistle of James continually calls us further into action because God's grace alone will not propel us on an effortless glide to holiness. We cannot just put the car in neutral because God loves us and assume we will live life as He intended; it is our active obedience in response to His grace that will keep us moving forward. Where there is grace to receive, there are also commands to obey. As our head understands and our heart is aligned, so our hands and feet need to respond, and James was not short of advice to share.

These verses give us some clear guidance:

- **Submit to God and resist the devil (4:7)**
- **Come near to God and He will come near to you (4:8)**
- **Purify and humble yourself (4:8–10)**
- **Do not judge or slander others (4:11–12)**
- **Do not boast or think you're in control of life (4:13–17)**
- **Do not hoard your wealth (5:1–6)**

Even in summary, this advice is far reaching and impactful. Imagine if every Christian in the world was able to stand firm and flourish in these areas – the church would undoubtedly be transformed. So how can we grow as we face these challenges? James is here to help us.

As we *submit* to God we also need to *resist* the enemy of our souls (James 4:7). To remain strong and steady we must pay attention to both. It's a bit like stabilizers on a bike: we must make sure that both wheels are on the ground to keep moving forward, and they will prevent us from falling over. So if submitting means actively aligning ourselves with God and His kingdom, resisting means refusing to allow the devil to get a foothold in that kingdom. We cannot live in freedom, running on the beautiful green football pitch of God's grace, if we then play the game by the enemy's rules. To enlist in God's purposes, we must resist, and if possible neutralize the temptations and distractions around us. My own experience is that the more I pursue God and His plans, the more I can expect to be pursued by an enemy who loves division among believers and distraction from our heavenly Father. Discipleship is a battle and we must fight it courageously with all the spiritual resources that have been given to us in prayer, fasting, and spiritual discipline. As we make that stand, James reassures us, the devil will flee; he has little room to manoeuvre where God is in control.

To reinforce the point further, and to help us to avoid getting too cosy with the enemy, the next instruction is key: James 4:8 tells us that as we come near to God, He will come near to us – which is surely one of the most wonderful promises in Scripture. It's worth noticing, though, that the ball is in our court. Most of us would, if we are honest, love to reverse this promise – we would prefer for God to show up first, with the hope that when He does, that would give us the kick we need to draw close to Him or to do what He has asked us to do. But that's not what James says. Our heavenly Father is ready and willing to lift us up and to strengthen us, but He wants a living relationship with us, a partnership where we actively participate without coercion. Being a brave and determined disciple means taking the initiative, stepping out in faith, trusting, and deliberately creating room for God to rule and reign in every area of our life. As we do so, God will reveal Himself to us, guiding, answering prayer, speaking through His Word, and bringing freedom. And so the virtuous circle of a faith relationship continues.

Submission in Action

None of us, however, can draw close to a holy God casually, without some self-examination. We have already highlighted the priority of purity for believers, but James now links in verse 8 the washing of our hands (our outward actions or behaviour) with the purifying of our hearts (our inner motives). We should, he is saying, genuinely grieve over our sin and remember that what we do is always motivated by who we are. What is hidden will ultimately always lead to what is seen. It is probably not that fashionable to talk about sin or prayers of confession; they don't make us feel that comfortable, after all. But it is a shame because holiness and keeping short accounts with God are at the heart of keeping our souls fresh and free from spiritual debris. As part of my daily routine, I often ask God before I go to sleep to highlight the areas where I have fallen short that day. He always seems to find something to nudge me about. Sometimes it is an action (or conversely a lack of action), and sometimes it is an attitude that has leaked out. As I confess what the Holy Spirit gently reveals to me, I then know I can sleep in peace as God reminds me that His mercies are new every morning and that His love is constant. Seeking to have both clean hands and a pure heart is about being practically and spiritually engaged in whole-life discipleship.

This chapter continues by extrapolating what living in humble submission actually looks like in practice by giving us three litmus test areas for us to consider. Pride, of course, is the main challenge to humility or submission, and that is the battle James is highlighting here. It can be perennially difficult to spot arrogance or pride in ourselves (yet surprisingly easy to observe in others), and yet it is an attitude that is in direct conflict with the humility James is encouraging us to adopt. If we are not careful, the things we do and say very quickly place us back in control, denying Christ first place in our life. This means keeping a careful eye on these areas James identifies as particular potential pride pitfalls:

How we talk about others. Sim has helpfully explored James' teaching on the power of words and how we master our tongue in chapter 3 of the epistle. But here in chapter 4 James is asking us to note the attitudes that lead to our words. Many of us have caught ourselves unwittingly making ourselves look better by making somebody else look worse. When we are judgmental – making decisions or assumptions about others and discrediting them in the process – we are in effect attempting to usurp God's position as the all-knowing judge in the process. It's as if we know best about everybody concerned. The converse is also sometimes true – we elevate others into the position of an idol, denigrating ourselves and God's workmanship in the process. Either way, we are getting it wrong and need to regain a divine perspective on the value of others and ourselves. We are not the ultimate judge; God is. It is possible to critique without being critical and to disagree without being disagreeable. We are all God's precious children and deserve to be treated as such.

A phrase we use a lot in our church is OFM – meaning One Fact More. Sometimes, when we make assumptions about a person, one more piece of information would shed much light on the situation. Why was that man rude to you this morning? Perhaps he has been made redundant this week. Why was that person so late? In fact, they stopped to help somebody who had fallen over. We love it when others give us the benefit of the doubt, so it is worth applying the OFM principle to others and to assume the best before we judge too harshly, because Jesus warns us (Matthew 7:2) that we will be judged as we judge others, and the measure we use will also reflect on us. That ought to stop us in our tracks for a moment.

How we plan our future. Do we ever secretly think we are masters of our own success and destiny? It is not bad to plan, to use a diary well, to save money for the future, or to have goals. But confidence creeps into pride if we think all the keys to our future are held in our hands. Applying our imagination, abilities, and exerting effort can take us a long way, but the question is whether it is God's way. Verses 13–17 of chapter 4 offer a great visual reminder that just as mist disappears, so our plans can easily evaporate. Humility means giving up our right to be right and acknowledging that things don't always work out as we assume they will.

The wonderful truth is that God will always be with us, whatever unfolds and however unexpected it is. When we plan with Him and submit our dreams to Him, our lives are open to divine direction. Who could fail to be inspired by previous generations of Christian missionaries and leaders, such as Catherine Booth who co-founded The Salvation Army alongside her husband William, and who is said to have stated, "I know not what He is about to do with me but I have given myself entirely into His hands." As faith-filled and focused as Catherine Booth was, this kind of surrender is not just reserved for those whom we might label as superheroes of the faith; God is asking all of us to live with brave abandon wherever we serve and wherever He leads.

How we deal with wealth. Similarly to Jesus, who spent a great deal of His time speaking about money and possessions, James in 5:1–6 has some direct things to say about how we handle our wealth. Our perspective on our possessions is a clear challenge to our humility, as they potentially give us a false sense of control and even corrupt our hearts. Losing our grip on stuff in a consumer-driven world is a serious challenge for us all, but in Matthew 6:24 Jesus stated that we cannot serve two masters – God and money. James pulls no punches in these verses, likening us, quite graphically, to turkeys fattening themselves up ready for their doom, unaware of what is going on around them.

How we steward our resources, seeking to remain generous, compassionate, and ethical in a materialistic culture, is a real opportunity for Christians to be distinctive. Our attitude to our finances and possessions is an important indicator as to who is pulling the purse strings of our life. Some of us might need to go back to our bank accounts and take a look at where our money goes and where our priorities evidently lie. Maybe we need some help with budgeting or some extra support if we have found ourselves in financial difficulty. Do we even know where our money is going? Perhaps the very thought of finance gives us feelings of anxiety rather than freedom.

Learning to handle our resources is a skill we can all learn and help each other with, if we are willing to be vulnerable and brave. But we need to ask ourselves the tough questions about how we feel about money in our heart. If we find it hard to give money regularly to our church, is it because we do not feel in control of where it goes? Has even our giving become a kind of shopping – where we give when it makes us feel good and withhold if it suits us better? For many of us, we can grow deeper in this and become more disciplined and generous. And as we do, we will experience the joy of giving at a deeper level as a result.

I have a theory that many church leaders go to bed and dream of what would be possible in their community and further afield if their congregation members were to give close to the 10 per cent tithe from their earnings that is often suggested. I remember one leader suggesting to me that our wallets are often the last part of us to become converted, which was amusing but probably true. Our money does have a mysterious power over us, and we are often defensive, proud, or embarrassed about it. I wonder what God might do if we managed to break this pattern and help each other to follow Jesus in this area.

To be transparent with you, this hasn't always been easy for me. I remember being a new believer, living on a student grant in a room covered in mould and being challenged by a gracious older lady living on her pension to give my portion to God. I thought she was a bit of a zealot at the time so I asked others for advice, thinking they would give me permission not to give my precious pounds away. But my new Christian friends encouraged me to start small with holy habits and to trust God – and wouldn't you know it, as that wonderful lady promised me, God has never let me down. Since we have been married, Mark and I have always aimed to give our complete tithe to our local church, which is such a blessing to us. I am so grateful for the way our church loves our family, our community, and the numerous overseas projects we support, and I want to be part of that financially as well as in every other way. But we also love supporting individuals and organizations, as we are able to, in addition to our church commitments. And on top of that giving, we also have a fun separate account where a small amount of money goes each month, building up gradually so that it is available to sponsor people, bless people, or respond to other God prompts.

We are not perfect (obviously), and it has not always been easy. We have had seasons of having enough resources, and we have lived by faith (and on baked beans) in the past too. But Mark has a great head for numbers, we budget very carefully, and we genuinely enjoy seeing what our money can do.

When we had children, we were keen to help them to get on track with this and we gave them three pots in their rooms, labelled Spend, Save, and Give. Their pocket money has always been divided into those three jars and they have loved taking part in giving to our church and other good causes. They have never slipped into the mindset of thinking their money is all theirs and for them alone to enjoy. But let's be honest, for children and adults, holy habits never just happen, and cracking our control over our money takes special attention. None of us finds this easy, but we can and should help each other with it. I am often inspired by generous friends (some of whom are well resourced and ridiculously philanthropic and others who are less well resourced and still generous in beautiful ways), and as a person in "ministry" I have often been on the receiving end of generosity as well. The joy and freedom of giving is definitely contagious, as is the temptation to hoard. It's worth spending time with people who get excited about what God can do with what He has given them. That doesn't mean we should boast in our giving, just as we should not boast in our spending, but we can celebrate and encourage each other in this vital area.

Making Holy Choices

Fundamentally, James' words here in chapters 4 and 5:1–6 are asking us very directly to think about the bigger picture of who is in control and how that expresses itself; to earn ethically and share generously and release the kingdom of God into the world as a result. We must remember what we have in our hands today. As refugees continue to flee for their lives, leaving everything behind, and as grandparents in Africa feed their adopted children scraps of food, our relative wealth can become a barrier that cocoons us from the needs of others. The book of James challenges us to be brave and determined about our attitudes and our actions, and that includes what we do with our money and possessions. The potential would be enormous if we could loosen our grip on our stuff.

James' encouragement to have clean hands and pure hearts and to externally live out what we internally believe is not only an issue of honouring God, but also a clear declaration to the world that we are marching to the orders of a different King in an altogether more glorious kingdom. Surrendering our all to Him and losing our place on the throne is far from being passive or fatalistic; as Christians, when we pledge our active allegiance to Christ, to following Him or to "lose it", we are making an intentional, decisive, and disciplined decision which leads to true and everlasting life.

The consequences of this *should* be clear for all to see. This challenge at the heart of this chapter is where the rubber really hits the road. Who is really in charge of our heart and how does that affect our decision making in practice? For example, if we are married and invited for an intimate coffee with somebody we know we are attracted to, we must make the wise choice and walk away – the cost of losing face now is minuscule compared with the cost of losing a marriage later. When given a promotion opportunity, we must weigh up the pros and cons responsibly, prayerfully considering what the extra influence and resources could do for God and others as well as any negative impact on our time, our autonomy, our priorities, and our relationships. When planning our monthly budgets and organizing our diary, we must ask God for His wisdom, remembering the poor, the church family to which we are called, and those who need our support.

On a different level, as we invest in relationships with our brothers and sisters in the faith, when we could easily "share for prayer" what is not ours to share at all, we should resist the temptation to gossip and instead pray for them faithfully ourselves. We must choose to build up the body of Christ (including our leaders) with kind and encouraging words, however and wherever we can, and deal with conflict in the most constructive way possible. When we leave church on a Sunday, we must then seek to live from Monday to Saturday in a posture of submission to Christ, knowing that we are all people of influence whose words and actions are always an overflow of our hearts, where the battles are lost or won. We are called to be whole-life disciples who live for Jesus, empowered by the Spirit wherever we are.

CHANGING THE ATMOSPHERE

In summary, I remember somebody once challenging me about how to live out my faith in a way that was distinctive and determined. This person put it to me that I had a choice: I could either be a thermometer or a thermostat. A thermometer, this person explained, simply tells you what the temperature is. It reflects what is around it but does not make a lot of difference. A thermostat, on the other hand, sets the temperature. It changes the climate and everything around it adjusts to the temperature it sets.

We can reflect the world around us like a thermometer, simply mirroring the surroundings we are placed in. But the book of James is, I believe, encouraging us to be more like thermostats. As we set our minds on Christ and bravely remain steadfast to that decision with the Holy Spirit's help and empowering, so we will find that the climate around us changes. People notice a change in the temperature; it just feels different. Folks know when they walk into a church where they are truly welcome. Friends know when they are being shown unconditional love and are forgiven for their errors. Colleagues are blessed when they receive generosity or words of encouragement that are given freely. People almost always respond with gratitude to prayer, to kindness, and to the kind of "greater grace" we have received ourselves. Our faith changes the climate, not just for us but also for others who do not yet know Christ. As such, we should always be prepared to provide them with an answer about the reason for the hope we have found (1 Peter 3:15). When the climate is right, good things grow and we determine the temperature around us, wherever our sphere of influence might be. Perhaps we sometimes underestimate the difference we can make as we are filled with the Holy Spirit and available to Him in our everyday life. The possibilities for us as we step up and step out into His purposes are more than we could ask or imagine.

James' passionate letter to his brothers and sisters leaves us in no doubt that being a passive disciple is a misnomer. It is simply not possible. God's sufficiency necessarily leads to our responsibility. As Christians, we are followers or apprentices who are being transformed to bring transformation to others. We have signed up for a dynamic and sometimes disruptive process of sanctification. Faith truly is an adventure, and we need to be brave as we seek to be obedient. As we prepare ourselves for all that that entails, we must loosen our grip on things that will hold us back and deliberately turn away from the kind of dissension and desires that weigh us down like unwelcome baggage. Instead, we have been called to wholeheartedly pursue a godly life that creates peace with ourselves, unity with others, compassion for our world, and restoration in our relationship with God. Our worship-filled response to God's unconditional love and grace should be far more than singing; it should be a life of determined and faithful obedience.

- If we think of "submit" and "resist" as two stabilizers on a bike, what does it look like when we get out of balance, not leaning far enough in either direction?

- How do you feel about prayers of confession? How do you tend to approach God? Communion/Eucharist is an excellent way of us coming close to God and then receiving from Him. Could you do this more as a family/small group/church?

- In the areas James highlighted – being judgmental, trying to control your future, and managing your finances/ resources – where is your biggest challenge to true humility? How do we guard against taking back the reins?

- Is there room for growth in your generosity? What was your immediate response to reading the section on finance? Discomfort? Defensiveness? A need for help? A desire to do more? How can you keep growing braver here? How will you build holy habits of discipline but also excitement about giving?

- Exercise: can you do a financial audit? Track your bank account for three months and see what is being spent where. Pray about how to reflect your faith with what you have been given and get help, support, or accountability if it would help. Talk to your church treasurer about how the church spends its money and how you can help (including Gift Aid) if that would be useful or inspiring.

- You could have a look at some of the following websites:

   www.capuk.org for their money course

   www.stewardship.org.uk to learn about giving more efficiently

   www.moneysavingexpert.com for lots of advice on how to make your money go further

   www.moneyadviceservice.org.uk (or others) for making a budget and financial planning.[41]

- An independent advisor or a friend you respect might also be helpful.

- Exercise: what do you love? Shopping? A nice glass of wine at the end of a hard day? Vegging out in front of the television on the weekend? Can you give that up for one week? How else might you spend that time/money? What did you learn about yourself at the end of the week?

- Would you describe yourself right now as more of a thermostat or a thermometer? How can you change the temperature around you to reflect more of God's values and passion for people?

- How do you feel about signing up to the adventure of losing your life? How committed are you to finding the greater life that Jesus offers, even if it is costly? Maybe now is a good time to pray a prayer of surrender again, giving your life to God's best for you.

Further Reading

John Ortberg, *The Life You've Always Wanted* (revised edition, Zondervan, 2002)

Philip Yancey, *What's so Amazing about Grace?* (new edition, Zondervan, 2002)

Christy Wimber, *Transformed* (Oxford: Monarch Books, 2017)

Nathalie MacDermott, *Dare to Trust: Choosing a Life of Risk* (Oxford: Monarch Books, 2017)

Gordon MacDonald, *Ordering Your Private World* (Thomas Nelson Publishers, 2007)

Bill Hybels, *Simplify* (Hodder & Stoughton, 2015)

Tom Wright, *Simply Christian* (SPCK Publishing, 2006)

Thomas à Kempis, *The Imitation of Christ*

Tim Keller, *Generous Justice* (Hodder Paperbacks, 2012)

Shane Claiborne, *The Irresistible Revolution* (Zondervan, 2006)

Rob Parsons, *The Money Secret* (Hodder & Stoughton, 2009)

Jen Hatmaker, *7: An Experimental Mutiny Against Excess* (Broadman & Holman, 2012)

Testimony from Chris, 60, Bristol

I chose to resign from a high-level job over an ethical issue. I had no job to go to and a six-figure mortgage, and interest rates were 16 per cent at that time. I had two children under four and my wife was working in the voluntary sector. I have also spent time being self-employed without knowing where the next month's mortgage payment or food was going to come from.

I did it because I believed I was following God's call. He drew my attention to Hebrews 10:32–38:

Remember those earlier days after you had received the light, when you endured in a great conflict full of suffering. Sometimes you were publicly exposed to insult and persecution; at other times you stood side by side with those who were so treated. You suffered along with those in prison and joyfully accepted the confiscation of your property, because you knew that you yourselves had better and lasting possessions. So do not throw away your confidence; it will be richly rewarded.

You need to persevere so that when you have done the will of God, you will receive what he has promised. For,

"In just a little while,

he who is coming will come

and will not delay."

And,

"But my righteous one will live by faith.

And I take no pleasure

in the one who shrinks back."

But we do not belong to those who shrink back and are destroyed, but to those who have faith and are saved.

When I was at university I was given a solid foundation of Bible knowledge and discipleship by The Navigators. It has helped me to be brave, to trust God, and to share my faith.

Knowing Jesus has changed everything. He has transformed my whole being, my thinking, how I live, my ambitions, my family, and how I speak and act.

You will never be able to outgive God, so I believe in living generously in every aspect of your life, toward God, toward your family, friends and work colleagues, with all your resources.

MEET CRIS ROGERS: interview by Cathy Madavan

Cris, you haven't always been a vicar living in the East End of London. What has brought you to where you are today?

Beki and I lived in West London working for Soul Survivor Church in Harrow for a number of years. Having had a great time seeing young people come to faith, we had also become dissatisfied with not seeing a group of hard-to-reach young people encounter Jesus. The more we read the Gospels, the more we saw how Jesus went to the abandoned places, to those on the edges, and to those not reached. If Jesus was the best rabbi in town, He certainly went to those often not engaged with. I would certainly never claim to be a good rabbi, but it did challenge me to think about where we located ourselves and who we were with. The more we thought about this, the more we felt called to go a place where people were often not engaged or left feeling on the edge. I suppose we felt the call to go to unreached people groups. For us that was an area that is 65 per cent from Bangladesh to a neighbourhood high on deprivation in East London.

You say you're not a good rabbi but people call you Rabbi Rogers. Why is that?

It's all to do with school. A couple of friends liked the way Rrrrrabbi Rrrrrogers rolled on the tongue. So it was a nickname from a particular group and it stuck. In their mobiles I'm still known as such.

Are there some things about you or your family that are unusual?

We are all passionate lovers of the science fiction films *Star Wars*. This isn't just something I love, but Beki and the kids too. We love dressing up (often called cosplay) and going to Comic Con, a huge pop culture conference twice a year. It has taken a number of years for us but we are happy to call ourselves science fiction geeks. I am also a member of a group called the 501st Legion of Stormtroopers. We visit hospitals and events dressed as characters from *Star Wars* to raise money for charity and put a smile on kids' faces.

We also love creating and making as a family. We have an activity we do as a family called the #Crafternoon. Often on a Friday we will be making, building, gluing, or creating something fun.

Have there been particular moments or seasons where you have needed to be especially brave?

I think the move to East London to follow a calling to a church which at the time had fewer than ten people. Leaving friends and a community that loved us was hard. We had to be brave as we relocated to a place with many community issues and challenges. There have been many moments of bravery when we have had challenges on our doorstep and incidents in the street that have left us wondering about our young family's safety.

What are the main challenges around making disciples in your church?

We are in a neighbourhood where commitment to anything is low. People feel like they don't fit and that others are constantly judging them. Reading levels are lower than average and the community is predominantly Muslim. Discipleship is a massive struggle. We have seen people come to faith but then not make the commitment to see their lives deepen and grow as disciples. We have been challenged to rethink how we disciple people in our setting, to create new pathways for discipleship that don't fit the standard middle-class culture.

How do you continue to be a determined disciple of Jesus when life can be so busy and demanding?

It's a daily decision to keep investing in my relationship with God. If I only went to see my wife once a week you would say that wasn't a marriage, so why does my relationship with God centred on Sundays? God has more for us than one day a week. I have a great mentor who has been challenging me to think about how I invest in my walk with God. How do I take responsibility for my own growth, feeding, and nurturing rather than expecting others to do it for me? I'm realizing that if I'm trying to be committed to an "idea" I constantly need convincing that it's a good idea, but if I'm trying to be committed to a person I need to spend time with that person.

FINISH IT

CRIS ROGERS

Be patient, then, brothers and sisters, until the Lord's coming. See how the farmer waits for the land to yield its valuable crop, patiently waiting for the autumn and spring rains. You too, be patient and stand firm, because the Lord's coming is near. Don't grumble against one another, brothers and sisters, or you will be judged. The Judge is standing at the door!

Brothers and sisters, as an example of patience in the face of suffering, take the prophets who spoke in the name of the Lord. As you know, we count as blessed those who have persevered. You have heard of Job's perseverance and have seen what the Lord finally brought about. The Lord is full of compassion and mercy.

James 5:7–11

We have been walking through the book of James, realizing the call to a determined disciple life. This life calls us to FACE the new person Christ is calling us toward, to LIVE out this life committed to Christ, and to allow Christ's work in us to TAME what needs dealing with and LOSE what needs to be left behind. We now come to the final section of James. A section that calls us toward a discipled life that aims to FINISH IT well.

In the previous chapters, we have taken the predominant theme from each chapter of the book of James as the main content. This means some of the chapters have been singly themed. The final chapter of James covers a number of major issues we need to address to FINISH IT. The call to disciples is to finish our race well even when life is difficult. It's in the drawing together of a number of threads that we can practise finishing the race well.

We will be looking at three threads. First, being patient in our suffering. Second, the call to be people with patience that means we trust God and those around us. Third, the challenge to correct others and be corrected while drawing others to a life with Jesus. These three threads help us and others finish our discipleship journey well. It's in these themes that we can make sure we are finishing what God has set before us.

As we approach the final section of the book of James we are encouraged toward "patient discipleship". Patient discipleship is the practice of holding on even when everything looks like it is falling apart. James addresses patient discipleship in the face of Jesus' lack of return – "until the Lord's coming", he says (James 5:7). In other words, patience even when Jesus still hasn't shown up.

When life gets tough we often hear people say, "Well, you gave it a good go." We live in a culture that doesn't commit to commitment. Marriages are committed until they just aren't. (It's important to note that I am not referring here to abusive and destructive relationships where the best and most healthy thing to do is to walk away and finish it.) People are members of organizations until they feel it no longer fits. Commitment is at an all-time low.

But the life of a disciple is a call to commitment and patience. We are called to not jack it all in the moment it gets difficult. The book of James calls us to be committed, push through it, wait, and be patient with confidence.

We are to keep on keeping on.

The beginning of the Genesis story tells us that humanity was created to be in relationship with God, with each other, and with creation. When sin entered the world, these three relationships were broken. We no longer trusted God, we no longer trusted humanity, and we no longer lived connected lives with creation. But Jesus' death and resurrection – the good news – is the reconnection with God, people, and creation. This means that, as disciples of Jesus, we are not meant to do faith alone. A commitment to people (church) is an outworking of the good news and our discipleship. We are meant to do life together: actively praying for each other, confessing our sins together, and being one with each other.

A selection of verses from James 5 reads:

> **Be patient**, then, brothers and sisters, until the Lord's coming. See how the farmer waits for the land to yield its valuable crop, **patiently waiting** for the autumn and spring rains. You too, be **patient and stand firm**, because the Lord's coming is near. Don't grumble against one another, brothers and sisters, or you will be judged. The Judge is standing at the door!
>
> Brothers and sisters, as an example of **patience** in the face of suffering, take the prophets who spoke in the name of the Lord.
>
> My brothers and sisters, if one of you should wander from the truth and someone should bring that person back, remember this: whoever turns a sinner from the error of their way will save them from death and cover over a multitude of sins.
>
> *James 5: 7–10, 19–20 [emphasis mine]*

Patience is not simply something a few people have. It is the choice we all have to trust that God is good. When we become impatient, it is because we have stopped trusting and think our impatient longing will somehow resolve the problem. All too often our lack of patience is linked to our lack of faith in God: if we knew that He was going to sort it out and knew when He was going to do it, we would have patience. However, "Who has known the mind of the Lord?" (1 Corinthians 2:16), and so often it is in the waiting time that we grow and develop in our relationship with Him. Like all the discipleship principles, growing in patience is not necessarily easy, especially when we have been waiting for something for a long time. In this final chapter we will explore patience and standing firm as key discipleship principles for the church.

HEAD: PATIENT DISCIPLESHIP

It is useful to consider the reasons why the biblical writers chose to focus on particular topics within their books and the contexts they were speaking into. Writing something by hand took a great deal of time and cost money to copy. The writers were very careful with their imperative topics. It is worth remembering that the Bible writers wrote about what was important and topical at the time. They saw issues and spoke about them in context. What is interesting is that so many of those issues are still prevalent today. This is a major reason the Bible is still relevant to us more than 2,000 years later.

A key phrase found in James 5 is the word "patience". This must mean that it had significance at the time for the church that was waiting for Christ's return. We also recognize that today, in many ways, it feels more prophetic than ever. James obviously felt that being patient and standing firm were key issues for these new believers. However, he must have known these would continue to be issues for Christians through the ages.

The root word used for "patience" in much of the Greek New Testament is *hupomeno*.[42] *Hupomeno* can be translated as "to remain" or even "to remain under". For many of us, the stresses of life can be heavy to carry and can catch us off guard. Often, pressure of life can leave us feeling overwhelmed and worn down. This biblical Greek word paints a picture that can be helpful when life feels like it is coming down on us. One beautiful way of seeing *hupomeno* is like an umbrella when it is raining. In bad weather, we may choose to remain under the protection of the umbrella. It is the same with patience. When we are under pressure we may choose to remain under *hupomeno*, patience. James tells us to remain under patience, to be protected by it.

Makrothumia

There is a second word for patience used by the writer of James. In James 5:7 we see a specific term which we translate as "be patient": *makrothumia*.[43] It is actually two words which have been combined: *makros* and *thumos*. *Makros* translates as "far away". *Thumos* means "anger, rage, or frustration". Together they mean something along the lines of "hold far away your anger" or "place frustration at a distance". The anger exists but it is where we choose to locate it.

Are you going to allow anger to be present and close or hold it at arm's length? This understanding of patience is not about ignoring our anger or having a passive resignation toward it. It is choosing to be self-regulating and restrained. It's the holding of frustration in such a way that we are not controlled by a hasty retaliation even in the face of aggravation.

Fruit

As we find in Galatians 5:22, patience is a product or "fruit" of God's presence in our lives (ESV UK). Patience is a fruit of the Holy Spirit, whose character is birthed within us. Because of this, Jesus' patience becomes a kingdom reality in the lives of His disciples. It is this patience that sets us apart from the world. It's not a reality that comes easily, nor should it. Patience is the outworking of God's activity in our lives, and this activity takes time to be worked out in our head, heart, and hands. The easy route to patience will always lead us back to impatience. It is in the hard work of choosing to receive the Holy Spirit, taking time to rest in Him, hear from Him, and trust Him to change us. This process of seeing the Holy Spirit's fruit at work in us is a slow process; it's a daily growth process which needs tending in our lives.

As we wait on God, encountering His Spirit, patience develops into the fruit. We should not be surprised that God's outworking in this area is a lifelong discipleship issue. There aren't many of us who are naturally patient. Sometimes what looks like patience is nothing more than cheap denial. I have a friend who looks like a patient character on first viewing. Sadly, under the surface his patience is in fact a denial of the reality of a situation. He ignores situations and avoids dealing with things in a healthy manner. He believes that if we pretend situations are different, things may just change on their own. This is not a healthy biblical patience of holding a situation with the Holy Spirit.

God invites us through his Holy Spirit to overcome our natural reaction to stress with a supernatural one – peace. Patience is a reality within us when and only when peace is present. While we have a restless spirit, we will always behave restlessly, but a peaceful spirit will present patience within. It shouldn't be surprising that Jesus' first words to the impatient disciples post resurrection were, "Peace be with you." Just imagine for a moment… they had seen Jesus die a most gruesome death. They knew He had been laid to rest behind an enormous stone. Then they hear rumours of His resurrection. We can only imagine how excited they were by the prospect of these rumours and how overjoyed at the possibility. It was into this place of confusion that Jesus spoke peace. It was through an encounter with Jesus that peace became present.

Patient Until...

The writer of the book of James gives us a clear time to be patient: *until* the Lord's coming (James 5:7). This passage presents us with an anticipation. Our patience is filled with a joyful anticipation of Jesus. It is until the moment that Jesus is present that we must actively practise patience. When this moment comes, we will find our longings satisfied in the presence of Jesus. James continually reminds people of this new moment of Jesus' presence.

Be patient, then, brothers and sisters, until the Lord's coming.
James 5:7

You too, be patient and stand firm, because the Lord's coming is near.
James 5:8

Don't grumble against one another, brothers and sisters, or you will be judged. The Judge is **standing at the door!**
James 5:9 [emphasis mine]

In other words, He is coming soon. Our patience finds its place in longing for Jesus.

Like a Farmer

James provides an image to help explain this patience. James 5:7 (NET) reads, "Think of how the farmer waits for the precious fruit of the ground and is patient for it until it receives the early and late rains." *Think* is a great word to start that verse. It can also be replaced with *meditate*. James invites us to spend time pondering the image for a moment. It's an image that provides an insight into the kind of life God wants for us as we wait for Him.

To go deeper in this image, we can go back to the time of Moses and look at the difference in how the people in Egypt farmed and how the people of Israel farmed in the desert. In Egypt, the land was irrigated not by rain but by the water flowing from the Nile River. In the time of Moses, the Nile was considered a god in itself. For the Egyptians, the Nile was the provider of life. It was because of the Nile that people were able to grow crops and have access to a constant source of water – a rare gift in such arid climates. Egyptians would dig a cleaver ditch near a farm site where water would flow from the Nile. A farmer would open the ditch and water would flow on his command. His view was that water existed and bowed solely to his command. The ditch could be opened as easily as the kicking of a foot.

But in Deuteronomy 11:10 God says to His people in exile "The land you are entering to take over is not like the land of Egypt, from which you have come, where you planted your seed and irrigated it by foot as in a vegetable garden."

It had become too easy for the Israelites in Egypt. It was like turning on the tap. There was no need for patience. What they needed was right there, readily available. Farming in Egypt could be done with little faith in God. As the people moved eastward and settled in their new land, God wanted to teach the people about trust. It was through the provision of the daily bread – remember the manna in the desert – that God could show His people what trust and patience looked like. They needed God to act because they could no longer provide for their own needs.

God took his people to a new land, a land watered not by irrigation but by rain. The people now had to do as God commanded and had to trust that He knew what he was doing. They hated it; they wanted to be in control.

In the same way, God sometimes has to take us to the desert to show us what patience and trust really look like. It is a struggle because we want to be in control.

God promised His people that in the new land the rainy season would come at the proper time. So the new method of farming looked different. A farmer would need to prepare and plant before the rain came. He would cultivate the soil, plant the seeds, clear the weeds, watch the birds, and wait patiently for God's provision. There might be no hint of rain, but the farmer had to trust patiently that it would come. God had promised it. Sometimes the rain would be late, but the farmers trusted it would come.

When the rainy season arrived, it came with two rains. The early rain would come to soften the soil and cause the seed to wake up and begin to grow. The rain would then stop and time would pass. The farmer would yet again have to wait patiently. Eventually the second rains would come and cause the crop to mature. This process of farming required the people to trust and wait. Egypt had made them impatient. Israel was about learning to trust again.

We live in this version of Egypt. We live in a culture where things come right now. We order shopping online and it arrives within a day or so. We turn on the tap and water is there. Electricity makes the lights come on within a millisecond. We don't need to be patient any more because everything we need is right there when we want it. This way of life hasn't made us more productive, just more impatient. But God wants to teach us a better way than impatience.

Statistically, one in four of us will abandon a website if it doesn't load within four seconds. Four seconds! Talk about impatience. This is what we call a "First World problem". First World problems are scenarios we term as *problems* since we don't have any real problems. A few examples…

- **Too many clothes and not enough hangers.**
- **Too many computers in the house and not enough Wi-Fi to go around.**
- **Returning from Hawaii to find the DVR is 100 per cent full.**
- **Having to choose between the white or black iPhone.**

According to an article written by the Fast Company, titled 'How One Second Could Cost Amazon $1.6 Billion in Sales', 50 per cent of Americans wouldn't visit an establishment for a second time if they were kept waiting for any length of time.[44]

We live in Egypt, and the epistle of James is challenging us to live like the Israelites. Remember the farmer, he says. Remember how he has to wait. Remember that his patience is tested. Remember that at times the rain never comes as quickly as the farmer would like it to come. Remember that the farmer has to just trust or have sleepless nights. Remember that God gives the farmer what he needs when he needs it. Be like the farmer, James encourages. Trust God; be patient for His provision. In the same way that God promises rain to the farmer, so God also promises us Jesus' return. Be patient like the farmer.

We have to presume that even though farming in Israel was harder, it had to be better for the farmer's soul. God took His people to Israel because it pressed them closer into Him. As farmers in Egypt they didn't need God; they were able to source everything they needed in the fertile land. In Israel, they were in the desert, and in the desert they needed God to do a miracle every year. It must have been stressful, but it was what they needed to trust Him.

God often takes us to the desert to learn how to trust and be patient again. In the land of Egypt, man was king; he was in control; there was no need to trust, wait, and be patient. In the desert, the people of Israel needed the true King; they had to put their control and trust in the King of the Universe and wait and be patient for Him to provide what they needed in His timing.

Patience in the Face of Suffering

Having addressed the patience of a farmer, the writer of James now takes us deeper into patience. He wants to explore the question, "What about patience when everything is going wrong?" What if the rain doesn't come? Or what if the rain comes and wipes everything out? James now challenges us to be patient even when everything is falling apart. I recognize in my own life that patience is easier when I am not under pressure, but James asks us to explore patience when under the sustained pressure of life events.

When I was fifteen, I was away on a camping break with friends for a week on a clifftop in North Yorkshire. Toward the end of the week the weather turned and a large storm arrived. Over the last twenty-four hours the wind became gale force 10 and the rain hammered down. As the night went on we ended up hiding in a marquee for safety as tents were blown down and our possessions were blown into the hedgerows. Sitting in the marquee, we watched from a distance as the big top crashed to the floor when the beams holding it gave way to the wind. Possessions were lost, clothes were soaked, and there wasn't a single dry sleeping bags in sight. It was a long night… and bitterly cold. With no mobile phones to call home we had to just sit tight and wait until our parents came to collect us. That final twenty-four hours seemed to go on for months as we were convinced that the apocalypse had arrived. We were fortunate and had warm and dry homes to go to. However, for many people, disasters like this, and worse, are life changing. We only have to consider the hurricanes or earthquakes and other disasters we hear about in the news.

Whatever the level of suffering we find ourselves in, for God it is important and relevant. When we are in the middle of suffering, time seems to slow down and our patience can run thin. We find ourselves being impatient and desperate. When we feel this way, we try to resolve things ourselves by taking matters into our own hands. In times like this, the letter from James calls us to a new brave place where we trust that God is in control, a place where we realize that in suffering that we are to fall back on God with our despair and confusion, and continue to journey deeper with Him as our trust and patience grow.

Hang on, hang on, hang on. Let's just pause for a moment. Are we saying that we need to learn patience when we are at our most "patience deficient"? Surely that's not possible?

James realizes the response to suffering is all too often to be less patient, so he uses the story of Job as an example of somebody who went through agony but grew in his trust and patience with God.

The story of Job illustrates a disciple clinging on to God when suffering is at its most intense. Job is an unforgettable example of endurance in the face of suffering, pain, and grief.

James reminds us:

We count as blessed those who have persevered. You have heard of Job's perseverance and have seen what the Lord finally brought about. The Lord is full of compassion and mercy.
James 5:11

Let's revisit the story of Job for a moment. Job was blessed above every other person of his day. He was wealthy, he had the perfect wife and family, and everything seemed great. We presume he had a beautiful home with the best views. Job had made it. He had everything his heart desired.

We are told that one day Job, out of the blue, lost everything. He suddenly experienced devastation that would be front-page news. Job lost his wife and his kids were all killed when the house collapsed in a tornado. His property was raided, his camels carried off, and his servants murdered. He even experienced fire falling from the sky and all his sheep were destroyed. Job's health declined as he developed sores "from the soles of his feet to the crown of his head" (Job 2:7). Throughout this entire tragedy, Job had no idea what would happen next, nor why. I'm sure his patience with God must have worn thin. He must have been pushed to his limit. He must have wanted to give up.

But that was not the way of Job. He did not understand, but he knew everything was in God's hands. In his loss, suffering, and pain Job cried out to God. Even though Job exemplified for us patience and faith in God, he did not ignore his situation or live in a place of denial. He was honest with God about his feelings and frustration, but acknowledged God's sovereignty within it all. This example still speaks to us today. We, like Job, have permission to allow ourselves to be vulnerable and real with God and to cry out to Him in prayer. God knows our feelings anyway, but He waits for us to come to Him with them, to open up to Him about our pain and impatience. Job showed us that crying out is our way of being patient. Clinging on to God when the wind blows us beyond our own ability to hold on. James highlights Job's story at this point in his letter to give us a model of patient suffering without losing faith in God. Job was a wonderful source of encouragement for all, and still is today. James also reminds us of the end of the story:

> *As you know, we count as blessed those who have persevered. You have heard of Job's perseverance and have seen what the Lord finally brought about. The Lord is full of compassion and mercy.*
>
> **James 5:11**

What the Lord finally brought about was the evidence for Job's patience. Job's life was restored, his family life rebuilt, and his property and livestock regained. Job 42:10 reads, "After Job had prayed for his friends, the Lord restored his fortunes and gave him twice as much as he had before."

What can we learn from Job? What is James trying to reference in this moment? First, Job shows us that the patience to hold on is worth the wait in the end. It's a painful process, but it's worth clinging on. We learn that God is ultimately holding us and is at work. Second, when we are at the point of almost losing perspective and letting go, we must build up and strengthen our relationship with God by being honest and open with Him; we must let Him in, not turn Him away.

James encourages us not to forget Job. He held on and God didn't let him down. James prods the early Christians to do the same – to not let go and remember that God will not let us down.

Suffering, Patience, and Prayer

Having spent such a long time talking about patience in the face of suffering or difficulty, it would only be right to make sure we counter this with the call to pray and hold things in prayer. To *finish it* well we need to be patient and also prayerful. Prayer challenges us to cry out for what is not fair and OK about the world. We believe in a supernatural God who reaches out to our natural lives. To follow Jesus is to follow a supernatural God who exposes His disciples to signs and wonders of the kingdom.

The writer of James, having not spoken much about the supernatural life of a disciple, drops in a few lines to remind the early church to be people who pray for miracles. It's important to note that James probably doesn't mention this much as it wasn't a contentious issue for the church, but this doesn't mean it's not an issue for us. They were still in a place of seeing miracles regularly. We see this in the book of Acts, where the early church were seeing signs and wonders regularly. James 5:13–16 reads:

> *Is anyone among you in trouble? Let them pray. Is anyone happy? Let them sing songs of praise.* Is anyone among you ill? Let them call the elders of the church to pray over them and anoint them with oil in the name of the Lord. *And the prayer offered in faith will make the sick person well; the Lord will raise them up. If they have sinned, they will be forgiven. Therefore confess your sins to each other and pray for each other so that you may be healed. The prayer of a righteous person is powerful and effective.*

James speaks of three kinds of prayer in the passage.

Praying for yourself. James didn't provide an outline of what suffering might look like, but he encouraged people to pray in the midst of turmoil (James 5:13). Some of us may struggle to pray for ourselves, but James encourages us to do this.

Elders praying for the sick. James then invites the church leadership or elders pray over the sick (James 5:14–15). When someone is so ill they can't make their way to church, James encourages the godly and wise in prayer ministry to go and pray for a miracle with the person in their own home. The world "miracle" isn't used, but James clearly states that the sick should be prayed over. This kind of prayer is an active desire to get to where the sick are and to bring God into the suffering. Someone may be patiently suffering, and this is may not be God's desire for them. God may be inviting us to see a miracle in the midst of their suffering.

Praying for each other. This invitation isn't for a select few but for the whole family (James 5:16). We are to confess to each other where we have sinned and pray for miracles of healing. James reminds the church that the whole family get to enjoy praying for each other, not just the super-spiritual few.

So James makes clear that in the face of suffering we are to be patient, but also be faithful in prayer. Prayer is inviting God into the suffering and hoping for a change of situation.

Once we start talking about healing, many of us start to wave a red flag. We are rightly concerned about the "What if people don't get healed?" question. We worry about upsetting someone. A person may go away wondering why God doesn't care or feel that God isn't noticing them. Sadly, in this situation our fear can stop what might be a miracle for someone in need. There is a danger that our fear of no healing stops us hoping for a miracle. We must remember that we have hope in the face of fear. We must be people who pray passionately for healing while at the same time holding the tension of not seeing miracles every time. It has to be sensitively offered and carefully administrated so that if someone goes away without healing they do not feel judged or unloved.

What James offers here is a walk of faith that is real with suffering and patient when things aren't changing; and it is a call to be people who pray for miracles. A disciple needs both of these things to FINISH IT well. It's praying for breakthrough that sets disciples apart from people who simply patiently ride out a situation.

This life as a follower of Jesus is that of holding the suffering with patience but also being people who pray for breakthrough.

Brave Patience and Brave Prayer

We have been thinking about the challenge to a disciple to be patient in how we finish the faith race well. Many of us have a long way to go. That means we need to think about how we choose to finish in a beautiful, godly way. I hope to have many years ahead of me so I therefore need to plan on running the race in a healthy way. Some things are going to take a lifetime to work out, while others may be sorted more quickly than I expect. James inspires us, through his reference to Job, to *be patient (makrothumia)*.

By not letting everything overwhelm us, we allow it to be held appropriately. Through God's peace and presence, we are to be people who don't become overwhelmed. Being patient means holding on well in the light of God's promises. We are also challenged with the place of prayer in the middle of suffering, to be people who hope that there is always going to be change through prayer and who will not lose the desire to see the sick healed. Finishing it means holding out patiently and praying passionately that God is coming close to us right here, right now, while also not seeing the breakthroughs yet.

This means we need to have brave patience and brave prayer. Brave in the face of nothing changing, or even of things getting harder, and brave to pray for miracles and breakthroughs.

This call to patience may be hard to make a reality in our lives. It might be that we struggle to even *see* how to become more patient. Standard psychology would talk about finding the triggers for our impatience and then managing the symptoms. It would say take a deep breath, count to ten, relax your body, manage your emotions. The reality is that we can try to manage our symptoms of impatience, but God wants to get to the heart of our impatience – which is control.

- **How does the farmer image James uses help us relate to waiting?**

Galatians 5:22 tells us patience is a "fruit" of God's presence in our lives. Are you able to "grow" patience in your life by investing in spending time with God? Why not take some time out to allow yourself to be fed by God? Jesus frequently went up onto the hillside to pray, to invest in this relationship. Many people have found taking a chunk of time to be in God's presence really helps. You might find taking time to retreat in a quiet place or connecting with God in worship helps provide you with a place to "be" in God's presence. Actively spending time with Him and allowing the Holy Spirit to be at work in you will bring about the fruits of Holy Spirit in your life.

- **Who around you encourages you to be patient in your faith? What is it about them that encourages you?**

- Could you find someone whose patience encourages you and seek to spend time with them? Why not ask them what helps them be patient? Ask them about what it is that their faith is placed in and how this has helped them endure.

This call to patience is a daily challenge to trust God's goodness. The writer of the psalms knew the challenges of life and the patience and trust needed to hold on to God's promises and provision when things looked bleak.

Here is a collection of passages that encourage us to trust, persevere, and hold on. Take time to read them. You could write them out and put them in a place where you know you need to be reminded to be patient. Is road rage an issue? You could print out a line of encouragement and stick it to your dashboard to remind you to pray when you are feeling frustrated and annoyed.

- Key psalms to mediate on:

  Read Psalm 37 and Psalm 27 and spend time reflecting on them.

- Shorter scriptures to mediate on:

  Meditate on the following scriptures. If it helps, copy or draw them out as a visual aid.

Be still before the Lord
and wait patiently for him;
do not fret when people succeed in their ways,
when they carry out their wicked schemes.

Psalm 37:7

Wait for the Lord;
be strong and take heart
and wait for the Lord.

Psalm 27:14

The Lord will fight for you; you need only to be still.

Exodus 14:14

Love is patient, love is kind. It does not envy, it does not boast, it is not proud. It does not dishonour others, it is not self-seeking, it is not easily angered, it keeps no record of wrongs.

1 Corinthians 13:4–5

Whoever is patient has great understanding,
but one who is quick-tempered displays folly.

Proverbs 14:29

Why not think through what your triggers of impatience are for a while? Are you able to name specific moments and the causes of your impatience? Take some time to place these in the hands of God. Our struggles find their proper place in Him as He helps us to carry what we carry.

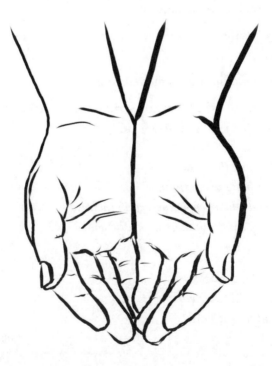

Cast your cares on the Lord
and he will sustain you;
he will never let
the righteous be shaken.

Psalm 55:22

Prayer

Lord, I bring to you my burdens and impatience.
You know my situation and my character defects.

You know I can't make it without You; I will always try to
control others and my situation without Your presence.

By Your grace, come and comfort and correct my heart.
Give me strength and perseverance to carry on,
trusting in Your loving control.

Amen

HEART: WHAT RULES OUR HEARTS WILL RULE OUR LIVES

You also, be patient. Establish your hearts, for the coming of the Lord is at hand.

James 5:8 (ESV UK)

The book of James helps us explore what the life of a disciple looks like. It challenges us to take a hard look at our internal life and the outworking of our faith. James encourages us to allow our faith to affect the way we live. Simple belief is not enough. Now the book of James draws to a close by calling us to an enduring race of discipleship, dedication, and finishing well. Committing to the way of Jesus is about *following* Jesus and *copying* Jesus to the finish.

Exploring the tongue has been a key image within the whole of the text. James recognizes that our mouths clearly reveal the state of our hearts. The dominant theme within the whole of the book has been that of the tongue.

In James 1:19 we learn that we should be "quick to listen, slow to speak and slow to become angry".

James 2:14–16 refers to the hypocritical use of words; words of comfort and help that don't become genuine helpful activity.

James 3 unpacks the message that teachers should be careful what they teach. Those of us who use words to build up should be aware that we will be judged for our teaching.

In James 4 we explore the abuse of the tongue within the life of the church in causing fights, using it to speak down and bring slander, and in worthless boasting about the future.

The focus of the final chapter is endurance and patience. Our patience is visibly worked out in our behaviour toward others and God. When we aren't patient we become people who are discontented with the now. Because of this, two things end up happening. First, our hearts grumble, and second, we try to take control by making things happen ourselves. James explores the outworking of this lack of patience by connecting it again with the use of the tongue teaching. He continues this theme by connecting lack of patience to control of the tongue through two areas:

- Grumbling (James 5:9).
- Publicly swearing or making over-the-top promises (James 5:12).

To finish our faith journey well, these two particular areas where patience is lacking become important for us to explore to be healthy and holy.

Grumbling

> Don't grumble against one another, brothers and sisters, or you will be judged. The Judge is standing at the door!
>
> *James 5:9*

As a youngster, I loved a good grumble. My dad used to call it "belly-aching." Like battery acid, grumbling and complaining eat away at whatever they land on. We all know someone who loves a good grumble. Their grumbling eats away at joy and dissolves all good outlooks. Spiritual grumbling has a toxic effect on us and the culture around us. We become impatient and we become bitter. We can grumble that God isn't active or grumble that others are not doing as they should. Both of these affect the way we look at the world and the way we want to interact with it.

Essentially, grumbling is about trust and the condition of our hearts. Do we trust others and do we trust God? Will God do as He has promised or are we likely to be let down? Grumbling is the outward sign of a heart bitter toward the activity of others and the activity of God.

Within the book of James, the word "grumble" is translated from the Greek word *stenazo*, meaning "having a heart that finds fault" or "sigh as the result of deep concern or stress". Does your heart have a bent toward finding fault, finding a problem, or feeling superior? Grumbling is actually about having a heart that believes we know what is right, what is best. We grumble when someone else is wrong and we believe we are right. The heart of grumbling is arrogance.

The solution to grumbling isn't simple but is possible with a change of heart. These steps will help us to conquer our grumbling habits:

- **Realize that grumbling is dangerous and will damage our hearts and attitudes.**
- **Trust that God is ultimately in control. We are just His partners.**
- **Let go of grumbling that has become bitterness and grudges.**
- **Focus on thanksgiving, not blame-giving.**

Just as grumbling reveals a bitter heart, thanksgiving reveals a contented heart.

Do Not Swear

James' teaching on swearing was a direct teaching from Jesus Himself. There was a practice in the Middle East at that time which continues to this day, where people would swear on things to give their words weight or authority. Rather than being people whose yes and no had decisive weight, they would have to swear on something. You may think this happens a lot in the West today, but imagine it in a much more demonstrative and loud way. People would swear on the temple or on the altar in the temple. A modern example might be someone who says, "I swear on my mother's grave," but this was more extreme. It had become so bad that people would string lines of these together. Something like this might be said: "I promise on the temple, I promise on the temple and the offering, I swear on the temple, the offering, the altar and the priest."[45]

My daughter would say it was a "pinky promise". James, like Jesus, challenges Christians to be people who are nothing more than clear and upfront. If something is a yes, just say yes. If it's not possible or wanted, then a simple no will do.

On top of having these long oaths, the Jews had developed more "tactical oaths", which appeared to promise something but had little real integrity. For example, a Jewish male could swear by the temple and have no obligation to fulfil the oath, but if he swore by the gold of the temple he was obliged. Jesus had something to say directly on this behaviour. Matthew 23:16–17 reads:

> *"Woe to you, blind guides! You say, 'If anyone swears by the temple, it means nothing; but anyone who swears by the gold of the temple is bound by that oath.' You blind fools! Which is greater: the gold, or the temple that makes the gold sacred?"*

This kind of solemn promise looks good on first appearance but in practice there is no real intention of it being kept. It is this behaviour that Jesus and James want to stamp out. James calls disciples to a behaviour that never needs to even take an oath because their word is always true. For a disciple, when we say yes, we should mean yes. Non-believers should never need further confirmation, as our words come with guaranteed truthfulness.

I was recently asked if I wanted to go on a strategy day for a charity I'm involved with, and I found myself responding, "I'll let you know." In the back of my mind I didn't want to make a full commitment just in case something better came up. Similarly, Facebook event invitations have discouraged me from being a yes or no person. I get an invitation and the "Maybe" option that is offered means I don't need to make a commitment. Maybe isn't a yes or a no; it's an opt-out from needing to make a commitment. We are in danger of becoming commitment-averse people. We struggle with the idea of making a commitment that might leave us unable to say yes to something else.

We see this playing out in all areas of our lives. Commitment to marriage is falling, commitment to working for one company for many years is dropping, and church attendance is still in free fall for those in their twenties and thirties. Many still attend, but they don't attend as often as they did because they have better options.

Commitment as a spiritual discipline can be a real struggle. Jesus says, "Let your 'Yes' be 'Yes'" (Matthew 5:37, NKJV). Our tendency is to try to keep our options open because options mean we're in charge, but when this option means we're not saying yes to the right things, then maybe we have a problem.

When it comes to our faith, there is a danger that we turn Jesus into an option too. We could say we love Him and want to follow Him, but we do it as a hobby rather than the first and most important thing in our lives.

In the third chapter of Revelation, there is a moment where Jesus says to the church of Laodicea, "So, because you are lukewarm – neither hot nor cold – I am about to spit you out of my mouth" (Revelation 3:16).

I wonder if Jesus would say the same to us. I'm not sure about you, but I feel a little ouch. Maybe He would say this to me. What if God responded to us the way we respond to Him – apathetic, slow, non-committal? The good news is that God's love is so much greater and more brilliant than that. There isn't a question about Jesus staying back. He's first in, He is present; He is with us, close by us. Thankfully, there is no complacency in God; He is active and dynamic.

The challenge is to be more like God. Maybe we need to stand up, step in, and make our response to Jesus active. Perhaps we need to say we're in, we're coming, we're open, we're ready, we're waiting. I wonder how dynamic our lives would be if we made God our first commitment, if we chose to place our lives first and foremost with Him rather than choosing the other options?

Jesus ends His rebuke of the Church of Laodicea with,

"Whoever has ears, let them hear what the Spirit says to the churches" (Revelation 3:22). I need to know that "maybe" culture is not Jesus' culture, and Jesus wants my commitment.

Patience and Commitment: the Condition of Our Heart

Patience and commitment show the condition of our heart revealed through our actions. Patience and commitment are both realities that are tested and seen rather than talked about. The epistle of James says that in the same way the mouth reveals our heart, our actions will also reveal our heart.

I heard a story many years ago. (Disclaimer: I don't know how true it is, but it stayed with me.) One day, a newly married couple agreed to meet up and spend time together shopping and having lunch. The man came out of work and patiently waited for his wife at an agreed location for fifteen minutes. He then continued to wait patiently for another fifteen minutes. As he waited he became impatient and kept checking his watch, calling and texting her to find out where she was. As time went on he became more impatient and angry.

Noticing a passport photo booth he had what he thought was a bright idea. He took a seat in the booth, inserted his coins, and then waited for the four photos to be taken. As the camera was about to flash each time he made the most angry and ferocious facial expression that he was able to muster. When the photos returned, they revealed how deeply angry he felt, and they shocked even him. He wrote his name on the back of the photo strip and handed them to a cash desk assistant. "If you see a young woman with dark hair, looking like she has lost someone, would you please hand her these." Then he headed back to work, happy that if a picture revealed a thousand words, he had preached a whole sermon to her. As I understand it, the wife still carries those photographs with her even today. When she is asked if she is married, she shows people the photos of her husband.

The expressions on his face in the photos showed his emotions for his wife in that moment in a very vivid way! The photos revealed what was in his heart. In the same way, our actions during the day can be like photos to others that show the state of our heart in that moment. We can profess love and care, but our actions reveal what's truly in our heart. If someone was to look at your life, maybe at a fixed moment in time, would it communicate a person of patience and love or of frustration and anger?

Toxic Culture

There is a toxic culture awash in the world where a lack of both commitment and patience are rife. Loyalty to any organization or group seems to be wafer thin. People make a commitment to something until something better presents itself. We exist in a culture that has developed a bad relationship with impatience. We want things right away and we want them only when we want them. This is ultimate selfishness. We have turned ourselves into the god of our lives rather than allowing God to penetrate all areas of our lives.

We have a tendency to see these characteristics in the younger generations. But I have spoken with people in their nineties who they say they see it in their children's generation too, but maybe not as distinctly.

Why is this? What is it that is causing us to not press in and give things the yes-be-a-yes that Jesus is calling us to? What is pushing us to grab control of our lives rather than trust in God?

This attitude reveals something about our hearts. James exposes what a heart fully committed to Jesus' way looks like. He highlights that our present culture, with its impatience, grumbling, judgmental attitudes, and the values of "maybe", "I deserve it", "the world owes me", is not Jesus' way.

The book of James is challenging us to allow our hearts to be penetrated to encounter a spirit that is different from the world. He calls us to a spirit of patience and perseverance and to align our hearts with the heart of God. We are told that "the Lord is compassionate and gracious, slow to anger, abounding in love" (Psalm 103:8). Remember that discipleship is *following* and *copying* Jesus, which means we must allow our hearts to become like the Lord's: compassionate, gracious, slow to anger, and overflowing with love. When we have a heart like this we cannot have a half-hearted life. A heart full of love, compassion, and grace is also a heart that is fully committed and fully invested.

Let's get real.

- **What is your heart invested in?**
- **What is your heart committed to?**
- **What stops you from following through on a commitment?**

To have a heart that is fully invested and committed is a discipline. There are times when we don't feel committed or we don't want to invest, but it is a discipline to allow our heart to be fully invested. When we have a lack of commitment, we are allowing our heart to run wild and devour whatever it wishes. There is a danger that we stroll passively through life, intrigued by a whole range of possibilities but not committed to making any of them a reality.

So what is the difference between interest and commitment?

- **Someone interested will read a magazine article or blog; someone who is committed applies what they have read each day.**
- **Someone interested procrastinates; someone committed focuses on getting the job done.**
- **Someone interested will make excuses as to why something is not possible; someone committed will work out solutions to make it possible.**
- **Someone interested will be involved when time permits; someone committed will live and breathe the project.**

There is a massive difference between a life lived for an interest and one committed for the long haul. Sadly, interests do not stick.

If this is something you are struggling with, it is worth asking, why are you holding back? What is stopping you from living the life that God has called you into?

So What Do We Do?

Shaping our lives so that we are countercultural, committed, and patient to stick in, press in, and be active in what God is doing is a challenge. However, it is a challenge that the Holy Spirit helps and supports us with, as we search our hearts and ask ourselves what is fuelling our lives and what are our core passions?

What rules our hearts will rule our lives. If *we* rule our hearts, we will ultimately wander away. We are quick to find a new *shiny thing* to captivate us. If our hearts are ruled by Jesus, corrected by Him and inspired by His kingdom, then we will find we will cling to Him. The church of Ephesus was doing all the right practices, but Jesus said to them, "You have forsaken the love you had at first" (Revelation 2:4). The church had neglected the intimate relationship they once had and replaced it with empty practices. This fledgling church lost touch with Jesus Himself, and replaced the focus with the routine of Christian life.

Only when we have been honest about who or what rules our hearts can we be honest in how we change things. What is ruling our heart?

When I have wanted to see things change in my own heart, I have given myself four questions to work through.

Question 1: Do we need to correct our mindset?

To be able to pull out all the stops and take real, quantifiable steps to live a committed life, we must first make a clear decision at the very core of our heart to hold nothing back. While we have a divided heart, we will have a divided life. Are we willing to hold nothing back at the core level of our being? To be able to move forward, we must make the decision that nothing is going to stand in the way of changing our heart.

Question 2: Are we willing to sacrifice what is ruling our hearts?

A life that is committed and patient is defined by the sacrifice that is made for this goal. Are we willing to make a sacrifice in order to run the race to the finishing line? Imagine a young runner who is devoted to training and practising each day. They put in time and energy to achieve their goal. Once we make the choice to be committed through sacrifice, it will translate into loyalty. Commitment takes sacrifice as it causes interruptions in all areas of our life. Are we willing to take the more challenging path that will interrupt us? Once we have corrected our mindset, we have to ask ourselves what we need to sacrifice in our life to live out that decision. Are we willing to let nothing stop us committing to living our life with God, and are we willing to allow this to translate into loyalty?

Question 3: Are we willing to invest in intimacy?

Any relationship needs to keep the fire burning. We all know that for a relationship to go the long haul it takes a lot of investment. A good marriage needs the fire of love to be stoked regularly. It doesn't happen without a desire on both sides. The strength of my marriage is only determined by the moment each day I choose to say yes to my commitment to my wife. In the same way, am I willing to commit to this decision to follow Jesus? Each day I have to make the decision to stay true to my big commitments, laying down today's commitment like a piece of a jigsaw. Remember the church in Ephesus? They had forgotten their first love. They had stopped investing in the intimacy, and Jesus called them back to that intimate place. Are we willing to be intimate with God today, and are we willing to put things in place to keep the intimacy up long term?

Question 4: Are we willing to keep on getting up?

Determination and commitment are deeply connected. Life is full of successes and failures. Inevitably, there are moments of setback and shortcoming in daily life. Without that regular determination to work through and overcome the setbacks, our commitment will inevitably waiver.

I have some great friends in recovery programmes such as Alcoholics Anonymous. They regularly talk about the problem of not being able to overcome the setback of the "slip-up": having a drink, or the slip up of using drugs. Even through it might only be one occasion, the slip-up can affect us, and the commitment to the whole can begin to waver. One failure can become a reason to give up. The key word in these moment is *resilience*. Are we resilient in the face of the obstacles? Being resilient in the long term involves becoming problem-solvers and moving to a place where we can take the necessary steps to navigate the barriers. A key mindset for resilience is being able to change our view of *problems* to the mindset of *challenges*. Problems will always leave us feeling overwhelmed, but challenges will leave us feeling invigorated and energized by the opportunity to grow and develop. Resilience and determination to keep on getting up after setbacks means we accept challenges as part of the landscape for our journey. Are we willing to keep on getting up and moving through the challenges for the larger goal?

Take some time to answer those questions yourself. Allow the Spirit to speak. These can be challenging but try and be as honest as possible.

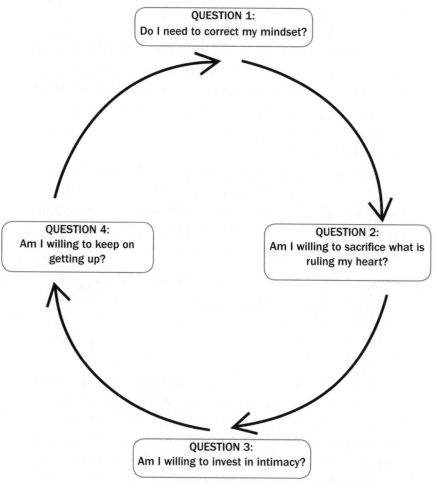

QUESTION 1:
Do I need to correct my mindset?

QUESTION 2:
Am I willing to sacrifice what is ruling my heart?

QUESTION 3:
Am I willing to invest in intimacy?

QUESTION 4:
Am I willing to keep on getting up?

HANDS: SAVED TO MAKE DISCIPLES

My brothers and sisters, if one of you should wander from the truth and someone should bring that person back, remember this: whoever turns a sinner from the error of their way will save them from death and cover over a multitude of sins.

James 5:19–20

We are called to FINISH what is before us, not to allow things to be left undone nor leave anyone behind. If this faith were a race, we are not called to run ahead and leave the weak behind. In this race it is not about the first across the line; it is about getting us all across the line. We are called to run alongside others and help them on the race, the strong helping the breathless, tired, and weary runners. Our job is to find those running off the track and help them back on the road.

You could say it like this: we are discipled to make disciples.

Something has to change in us because this patient, committed life of a yes-meaning-yes person also means being committed to God and committed to others. It also means we now have a commitment to the calling set before us.

> *"Therefore go and make disciples of all nations, baptising them in the name of the Father and of the Son and of the Holy Spirit."*
>
> *Matthew 28:19*

When we accept Jesus, we are called to follow Him, but we are also called to copy Him. Jesus was in the business of impacting people's lives by leading them to repentance and then to a place of transformation, and further still to a place of involvement. Finishing our faith, seeing it through, means not just giving ourselves to Jesus but also leading others to this place.

We Need Each Other

James made it clear that there is a community role for each of us. We are to watch out for one another and for those who need redirecting to the family.

It is not possible to be a disciple alone because we need others to lovingly confront us when we need challenging, and vice versa. We are meant to bring out the best in others and allow them to bring out the best in us. This community life involves keeping one another in check and allowing ourselves to be kept in check. This activity of having each other's back is central to what it means to be family. When people announce that they are still a Christian but they just don't go to church, we know it is not going to end well. Without the family holding each other up, supporting and cheering us on, there is no Christian faith. We cannot do it alone. We need the support of our brothers and sisters. Belief in Jesus without community discipleship is nothing more than belief. We don't *join* a church; we *are* the church, and this is not possible alone. It is this behaviour toward each other that makes church church.

Jesus is Looking for Disciple Makers

Jesus is looking for more than disciples. He also wants us to be people who make disciples. Replication is at the heart of the Jesus movement. We follow and copy others and others follow and copy us. Of course, this does mean we need to make sure we are a good copy of Jesus. You could say it like this: a disciple is a learner who is learning to learn, and our task is to help others learn to learn too.

Without this replication we will not see future generations of followers of Jesus. We might be the best church there has ever been, but without replication we have a problem. The call of a disciple is not simply to consume all God has for us but to stimulate life in others, to draw others back to Him, and to make disciples.

This call of reproduction is often seen as conversion, but it is so much more than that. Being a disciple is more than just being converted. It's moving beyond simple belief to a life that is defined by picking up the cross.

So what is the difference between a convert and a disciple?

- **We don't simply believe; we behave.**

- **We don't focus on rules; we focus on Jesus.**

- **We don't just turn up; we pitch in.**

- **We don't practise faith in our hobby time; we make time.**

- **We don't only read the Bible; we live out the Bible.**

- **We don't go to church; we are the church.**

The kind of disciple the book of James is calling us to is someone whose head, heart, and hands are fully following and copying the life of Jesus. A disciple is someone who heard Jesus' commission and mission and made it their mission too. Jesus' values become their values. Jesus' passions become their passions. Jesus' heartbreak becomes their heartbreak. It is this kind of life that Jesus wants us to replicate in others as we call them to reconnect with Him, each other, and creation.

The challenge for the church is that we have made conversion to faith about sin management and sin correction. We have told people they are sinners needing to be saved. This is it is only a portion of the gospel.

Jesus didn't just die to save us *from* something, but *for* something. Jesus died so that we might be free to become who we were meant to be. Discipleship is the exploration of finding out who we are.

Recently, I had a great conversation with a young guy about the gospel. He expected me to talk about sin and how he needed to deal with the issues in his life. The problem is, sin inspires no one. So I started with the beginning of the larger God story: creation. I told him how he was awesome. I told him he had been created to be fabulous and that God had created him with gifts, talents, and dreams that had been lost. I told him God had planted an image deep within him that meant God has so much on offer for him to do and be. He got excited. He didn't realize God not only had put gifts in him but that God in fact liked him. We talked at length about the dreams God had for his life and how God wanted to bring out the best in him. It was only then that we moved on to talking about sin and grace. So having heard that he was wonderfully made by a wonderful creator, and that this creator had gifts for him and plans for his life, he then began to see how sin in his life was in fact stopping him from being involved with what God had planned for him. So the sin needed to be dealt with if he was to ever live life to the full. As I sat with this young guy he realized that to become all that he was made to be, he needed to be forgiven. He accepted Jesus and responded to the gospel.

If we understand the full gospel – the gospel of God's creation, fall, redemption, and re-creation – suddenly sin needs to be dealt with.

- **CREATION: You were created to be with God to make, dream, and partner with God.**

- **DECREATION: Because of sin we have headed in our own direction and left God and His partnership behind.**

- **REDEMPTION: God comes in Christ to reconnect us to Him. His death for ours.**

- **RE-CREATION: God has saved us to once again partner with Him in His kingdom work. Life now becomes about partnering with God in His beautiful and brilliant work.**

The young lad's salvation came because he first realized who he was meant to be and then he realized his sin had stopped this from being a reality. He was gifted to bring about goodness in the world; he had wandered off track from this, yet Jesus brought him home. So what next? There was a job to *finish*, and this is where many of us get stuck. This young man's life was saved for the purpose of serving the

King, for a discipled life. His gifts and talents were originally given to him for serving the King, but he had squandered them, and now he was back to the beginning, ready to use them. Jesus doesn't just save us *from* something (sin), but also *for* something (partnership). A disciple-maker is someone who leads people to Jesus and then helps them live like Jesus in partnership with the King.

- What stops you from helping people to realize the truth that there is more for them in Jesus?
- Who made you a disciple? What can you learn from them?
- Who could you spend time with who might help you become more confident in sharing your faith?

This Discipleship is Inconvenient... Come and Die

When we read James' instructions to lead people from error and help the wanderers (James 5:19), this can sound judgmental and critical of others. I think there are two truths:

- Some of us are worried about upsetting our friends so we don't say anything about their behaviour because we want to avoided a hard conversation.
- Some of us are too quick to judge and speak up too fast. We make no friends and come across as arrogant religious Pharisees.

Neither of these is helpful. One never helps people who are off track and the other becomes a painful voice to listen to and so is avoided. We have to recognize the truth that we cannot make Jesus more convenient. Our culture wants to say we can have and believe all things and that there shouldn't be a clash between them. We aim to water down the call to discipleship in the hope to get more people *in*. Jesus is not looking for more people in, but more people giving themselves to Him. We cannot make following Jesus comfortable and easy because discipleship is about following and copying. You cannot copy Jesus and not be changed. We can't reduce the expectations for people in the hope they stay in a religious club. This call to follow and copy is costly. If we present people with a Jesus who is far too easy to follow, if we don't speak of our lives needing correcting, then we can't blame them for jumping ship when things don't go smoothly. Dietrich Bonhoeffer said it beautifully: "When Christ calls a man, he bids him come and die."[46]

Jesus spoke clearly to His disciples in Mark 8:34 when He said, "Whoever wants to be my disciple must deny themselves and take up their cross and follow me." In other words, if you want to go where Jesus is going, *follow* and *copy* Him and pick up your cross and sacrifice everything for Him. This is high cost, but it brings high transformation.

Please understand that it is imperative that correcting someone or helping to redirect someone should always be done with humility and compassion. Most of the heartbreak that I hear about in the church is when this has been done badly. People have been rebuked and hurt, not because of the message but because of how it was presented. I have found that many people simply need a word of support, an encouragement, and a friend. Sometimes we can stride in too quickly and miss the delicacy of a situation. I don't believe any one person wakes up and chooses to wander into error. It just happens over time, and over time they can be helped back. But the key here is *over time*. Things don't always move at the speed we want them to.

Correction Has to Be Done Carefully

Have you ever been asked to rank your greatest fears? I would imagine the fear of death would rank rather high. I would also imagine the fear of speaking in public would be high up that list too for many people. A loving friend who leads a church told me recently their greatest fear was having to confront someone who had wandered off track. I would probably agree with them on this issue. Having to confront and correct someone is hard, worrying, and difficult.

Correction Must Be Done Wisely

Although James challenges us to correct error, he doesn't give us clear steps how to do this. That's okay, because the whole of the Bible does. Paul writing to Timothy provides wisdom on how to navigate such situations:

> As I urged you when I went into Macedonia, stay there in Ephesus so that you may **command certain people not to teach false doctrines** any longer or to devote themselves to myths and endless genealogies. Such things promote controversial speculations rather than advancing God's work – which is by faith. **The goal of this command is love**, which comes from a **pure heart** and a **good conscience** and a **sincere faith**. Some have departed from these and have turned to meaningless talk. They want to be teachers of the law, but they do not know what they are talking about or what they so confidently affirm.
>
> 1 Timothy 1:3–7 [emphasis mine]

Correction must be done in love. Paul clearly told Timothy that the goal is one of love. Correcting someone is not a game of one-upmanship; it is about love and relationship. Timothy was already in Ephesus, invested and in relationship with the people. Our purpose is to love and serve one another. Paul told us that the tone of this must not love an argument. We can't correct someone and be antagonistic. We must be loving and invested in a relationship with them. This means our approach must be kind, patient, and gentle, but also firm. We don't love someone if we don't correct and help them. Leaving people to drift further into error is not loving, even if it feels easier.

Correction must be based on God's Word. Paul recognizes that there are some who want to be teachers but don't know His Word. We must make sure, when wanting to correct error, that we are correct and that our correction is biblical. Our correction has to find its basis clearly in Scripture. Anything else is personal opinion, and we have to be careful not to drift into our personal views rather than true biblical perspectives. Paul states that some have drifted into meaningless talk. The only way we know if we are doing this is by checking biblically.

Correction must be done in the awareness of spiritual warfare. Too often we approach error as if it is a natural problem. Scripture shows us that we live in a spiritual battle. This battle is raging not only in the spiritual but also in the natural world. Ephesians 6:12 reminds us that the battle is not against flesh and blood but against spiritual forces. Our struggle is against the work of the evil one, who sets out to separate and divide. The primary posture of the kingdom is relationship, but the primary challenge of the evil one is division. We must not play further into this division. This means that before we do anything we must realize that our greatest weapon against the work of the evil one is prayer. It would be foolish for us to not talk to God before we talk to people. Prayer must be the thing that saturates the whole process of biblical correction.

Let's be honest, many of us may walk away from Jesus at some point in our lives. We may not realize it, but gradually our thinking and focus may drift from Jesus. This can happen for all kinds of reasons:

lifestyle changes and challenges, allowing the world to influence our thinking, or just tiredness and weariness. This is where a good, loving friend is invaluable; to come along side another, gently challenge, and encourage is such a godly thing if it is done in the right way. If we don't look out and correct each other, then we will all end up in a mess. Without loving correction we will never be who Jesus saved us to be. We must love each other and speak to each other the way we first want to be spoken to ourselves.

If we are to be people who finish our faith adventure well, we do need to allow others to correct our course. Sometimes we have wandered into the scrub ground and we need correcting to get back on the path. This is often painful, but it is of utmost importance and worth reflecting on. Is the direction you are heading in for all areas of your life that of the direction of Jesus, or are you heading a little off course, or are you heading way off course? It's worth asking yourself a few questions.

- What aspect of giving biblical correction is the most difficult for you?

- Paul talks about "commanding" someone to stop teaching (1 Timothy 1:3). What would you say is the correct balance between being loving and kind toward someone and being forceful enough to make a clear point?

- Jesus rebuked the Pharisees and Paul rebuked teachers. How do we fit this with Jesus' and Paul's teaching on kindness and gentleness? Should we ever imitate the kind of rebukes we see Jesus and Paul do?

- If you personally needed to be corrected on an issue, how well would you respond? Would you be open to being challenged?

Further Reading

Margaret Whipp, *The Grace of Waiting: Learning Patience and Embracing Its Gifts* (Canterbury Press Norwich, 2017)

RT Kendall, *The Way of Wisdom: Patience in Waiting on God* (vol 2) (Authentic, 2005)

Tim Keller, *Walking with God through Pain and Suffering* (reprint, Penguin, 2015)

Sam Allberry, *James: for You* (The Good Book Company, 2016)

Tom Wright, *Spiritual and Religious: The Gospel in an Age of Paganism* (IVP, 2002)

Dallas Willard, *Renovation of the Heart: Putting on the Character of Christ* (TH1NK, 2005)

David Benner, *Desiring God's Will: Aligning Our Hearts with the Heart of God* (IVP, 2001)

Testimony from Pam, 78, Macclesfield

I've faced several challenges in life. I nursed my mother through terminal breast cancer while balancing a job as a social worker, running a home, and looking after two sons and a husband. Latterly I have had to face the fact that my husband of fifty-six years has Alzheimer's disease. He has needed to be cared for in a nursing home. Coming to terms with losing the man I married, his loss of memory, and learning how to cope with it all has been a challenge. Back when he was diagnosed there was very little in the way of practical help like clubs and groups. We floundered a bit.

However, with the help of friends similarly affected by dementia, and the support of my church, we decided to start our own group for people with dementia and their carers. We launched our Golden Memories group in 2015. We started with five couples and now we have more than twenty-five couples attending our fortnightly sessions. We are aided by volunteers who all bring their various talents and gifts to the sessions. The group fills a gap in the services provided for people with dementia and their carers. Most services cost quite a lot of money, but our fortnightly session is free and is supportive of both the carer and their loved one.

Since the start of our group, several other churches have been able to see how easy it is to provide this outreach to the community. As a result, many more people with dementia have been able to obtain support, help, and enjoyment from meeting together. To date, five new groups have been set up in the surrounding area.

I don't feel particularly brave, but whenever I am faced with a problem I turn to God and He gives me strength to carry on. The answers usually come as to how to deal with the things that worry me. I know he will never leave me nor forsake me.

Knowing Jesus means everything. He keeps me going when I feel down or sad and He helps me put everything into perspective. I count Jesus as my friend and confidant; I can ask Him anything and talk to Him any time I need to. He is my counsellor and my advisor, and He calms me down when I get worried or upset. Nothing is impossible for Jesus, and I know that He is in control.

I found Jesus when I was twelve years old. I went astray at times but I know He never let me go and I always found my way back to Him. What a friend we have in Jesus. My church family are such a support too, and I feel totally blessed.

THE FINAL CHALLENGE

CRIS ROGERS

We have been looking within this book at the call of discipleship, to follow and copy Christ.

Within the book of James we have been challenged to face the mirror of God's Word and the authentic discipleship it requires. We have seen how we need our identity, attitudes, and behaviour to be shaped by what God says about us and to us. As we listen and respond to Him, our whole lives will become more Christlike.

This means we now LIVE out this Christlike life. James calls us to the bravery of faithful service to God through serving the poor and vulnerable. We demonstrate our faith based on grace by the way we now live out our salvation, by becoming His hands and feet in the world.

The call to live like Christ means we are always going to have some work to do, which means we TAME the things in our lives that need taming and we LOSE what needs to be lost. What we say reveals so much of who we are. If we can learn to tame our tongue, we will be one step closer to living more like Jesus and embodying the wisdom that "comes from heaven" (James 3:17). This walk of discipleship is one where there are attitudes, desires, and wants that need to be sorted, trusting that Jesus has something better for us. God loves us too much to leave us as we are; He wants us to be free from the things that hold us back. As we deliberately lose the battle over who is in control of our life, we find both comfort and courage in King Jesus and His promises. It is surrender to Him that ultimately leads to peace. Leaving behind the baggage that weighs us down, we are then free to find life in all its fullness and grace in every challenge.

So then we FINISH it.

To finish a race, we have to be in the race. It isn't possible to be a sideline disciple. To finish means getting on the track and moving forward. Faith cannot ever be something that we just sit back and watch happen. Discipleship is a movement of following and copying Jesus. Are you up for the challenge to live for and *keep living for* Jesus?

When I was a child I played a game which I claimed one day would be an Olympic sport. The game was called "ghosting". The object of the game was to walk behind a stranger on the high street and follow them as closely as possible. Imagine standing inches away from someone in public and walking in time with them. The purpose of the game was to follow them closely but that they would never notice you. Over time I became quite good at walking inches behind a stranger. I have never been a sportsperson, but this sport was my chance at Olympic glory. I practised and became, in my mind, the best ghoster known to humankind. Sadly, nothing came of it and it was never picked up by the Olympic committee.

But I did become good at ghosting. On some occasions I could be ghosting someone for a few minutes before they noticed and the game would inevitably end with an embarrassing silence as a stranger stared at me. On one occasion the guy I was following just had no idea and it went on and on. After a few minutes I had a question to ask myself: see this through or just slip away and give up?

You're following and copying Jesus; you have been called to a life of discipleship. There will come times when this discipleship gets tough and some seasons when you might think about giving up. But this call to commit and see things through is the call of a disciple.

Are you willing to keep going? To keep Facing it, Living it, Taming it, Losing it, and Finishing it?

When a long distance runner is mid-race, they often talk about hitting a runner's wall. The wall is a moment where you want to give up because the challenge feels too tough. I would argue there can be a "discipleship wall" in the same way. Each of us will have moments where the pain of following Jesus becomes difficult. Our bones ache, temptation comes, or we feel let down. If you have never hit this, then bless you, but get ready, for one day it may come out of the blue.

We end here by giving you five tips for running this discipleship race well when you hit that wall.

What should a disciple if he or she hits the proverbial wall?

- **Get with other disciples.** Be with others who are passionate and on fire for Jesus. We can feel like we want some time off church or away from everyone else, but this is the opposite of what you need. We need community. Hell's strategy is to separate; heaven's strategy is relationship. Press into Christian community.

- **Put things in perspective.** It's easy to become disheartened and defeatist, especially when we have tripped up and fallen. When we make mistakes it's too easy to think we've blown it and to stop. We have to put the whole of our lives in perspective in the light of Jesus' death and resurrection. Take time to focus on the decisions you have made in the past that have been good and godly. Also put your life into the perspective of Jesus. Jesus died for you, for the whole of your life as well as for every little moment.

- **Identify your stress factors or your weaknesses that keep pulling you back.** We all have weaknesses which, if not dealt with properly, can cause us long-term stress and difficulty. This is why Jesus says, "If your eye causes you to stumble, gouge it out and throw it away. It is better for you to enter life with one eye than to have two eyes and be thrown into the fire of hell" (Matthew 18:9). Jesus is challenging us here to distance ourselves from the things that will ultimately let us down in the race.

- **Take a sabbath.** When things are tough, remember that God gave us the sabbath, a day to rest and be re-created. Re-creation in recreation. Our physical health affects our spiritual health. There are times when we need to take time to breathe in, to rest, to be restored.

- **Press in and keep training.** What we do in the quiet affects what we do in public. If you're hitting a wall, what you need is to take in something good. Runners talk about needing to press in, take in fluids. Our fluids are Scripture, prayer, and the Holy Spirit. A daily diet of Scripture, prayer, and the Holy Spirit will set you up well and make you less likely to hit the discipleship wall. But even if you do hit the wall, the best place to find yourself is back with Jesus, reading His words, hearing His words, and encountering His presence.

Final Prayer

As we draw this book on discipleship to a close, we want to make sure we take a moment to agree things into our lives. We have to say yes to this kind of life and actively give ourselves to it. At the start of each year, many Methodist churches join in with a covenant service where they do exactly that. They dedicate themselves to this whole life of following and copying Jesus. In this service they pray a prayer of dedication together.

Why not take this prayer and use it to dedicate yourself to this life today? As the words sit on the page, you might like to read them through. As you do that, consider which lines you especially wish to own for yourself. Once you have taken in each line, be encouraged to speak it out loud. By speaking the prayer out loud, a clear decision is being articulated to God.

I am no longer my own but Yours.

Put me to what You will,
        rank me with whom You will;
                put me to doing,
                        put me to suffering;
let me be employed for You,
        or laid aside for You,
                exalted for You,
or brought low for You;
        let me be full,
                let me be empty,
                        let me have all things,
let me have nothing:
        I freely and wholeheartedly yield all things
                to Your pleasure and disposal.

And now, glorious and blessed God,
        Father, Son, and Holy Spirit,
                You are mine and I am Yours.
                        So be it.

And the covenant now made on earth, let it be
ratified in heaven.

Amen

ENDNOTES

Chapter 1: Face It

1. Francesca Washtell, 'Britons spent £250m on unused health and fitness clothing last year, according to the 2016 Fitness Knowledge Report', City A.M. Available at: http://www.cityam.com/237653/britons-spent-250m-on-unused-health-and-fitness-clothing-last-year-according-to-the-2016-fitness-knowledge-report (last visited 6 December 2017).

2. 'Bristol named best place to live in Britain in 2017', BBC News, 19 March 2017. Available at: http://www.bbc.co.uk/news/uk-england-39320118 (last visited 6 December 2017). 'Top 10 Worst places to live in England 2017', iLiveHere.co.uk (last visited 6 December 2017).

3. https://en.oxforddictionaries.com/definition/narcissism (last visited 27 November 2017).

4. Rebecca Solnit, 'The Loneliness of Donald Trump', available at http://www.lithub.com (last visited 6 December 2017).

5. 'A personal statement from the Archbishop of Canterbury', 8 April 2016. Available at: http://www.archbishopofcanterbury.org/articles.php/5704/a-personal-statement-from-the-archbishop-of-canterbury (last visited 28 November 2017).

6. 'Body dysmorphic disorder (BDD)', NHS Choices. Available at https://www.nhs.uk/conditions/body-dysmorphia/ (last visited 6 December 2017).

7. Elaine Storkey, *The Search for Intimacy* (Hodder and Stoughton, 1995), p.25.

8. David Partington, *Kicking it: Eating Disorders, Pornography, Drugs, Alcohol* (IVP, 1991).

9. Stephen King, *Different Seasons* (Hodder and Stoughton, 2012), p.103.

10. William Barclay, *Gospel of John Vol 1 Daily Study Bible Series*, revised edition (Westminster/John Knox Press, 1975).

Chapter 2: Live It

11. Luther writes this in his Preface to the Epistles of St James and St Jude.

12. A. C. Myers, *Eerdmans Bible Dictionary* (Grand Rapids, MI: Eerdmans, 1987), p.551.

13. 'William Wilberforce', BBC Religions, 5 July 2011. Available at http://www.bbc.co.uk/religion/religions/christianity/people/williamwilberforce_1.shtml (last visited 6 December 2017).

14. Nicky Gumbel, Twitter, 12 August 2017. Available at https://twitter.com/nickygumbel/status/896468650244403200 (last visited 6 December 2017).

15. John Stott, *Christ the Controversialist* (Tyndale Press, 1970), p,51.

16. Josiah Bull (ed), *Letters by the Rev. John Newton: Of Olney and St Mary Woolnoth. Including Several Never Before Published, with Biographical Sketches and Illustrative Notes*, (Religious Tract Society, 1869), p.400.

17. L. Ryken, J. Wilhoit, T. Longman, C. Duriez, D. Penney and D. G. Reid, *Dictionary of Biblical Imagery* (InterVarsity Press, 2000), electronic edition, p.615.

18. 'Statistics on child abuse', NSPCC. Available at http://www.nspcc.org.uk/Inform/research/statistics/child_protection_register_statistics_wda48723.html (last visited 6 December 2017).

19. 'On measuring the number of vulnerable children in England', Children's Commissioner, July 2017. Available at https://www.childrenscommissioner.gov.uk/wp-content/uploads/2017/07/CCO-On-vulnerability-Overveiw.pdf (last visited 6 December 2017).

20. Home for Good. Available at www.homeforgood.org.uk (last visited 29 November 2017).

21. C. Victor et al, 'Loneliness, Social Isolation and Living Alone in Later Life', Economic and Social Research Council (2003).

22. "Preliminary analyses from an unpublished meta-analysis of 240 studies suggests a 26 per cent reduced chance of mortality for married people compared to others (who are divorced, single, widowed etc.) after a follow-up period of just over eight years." J. Gierveld de Jong, M. Brose van Groenou, A.W. Hoogendoorn and J. H. Smit, (2009) 'Quality of marriages in later life and emotional and social loneliness', Journal of Gerontology: Social Sciences, 64B(4). Available at http://depot.knaw.nl/7520/ (last visited 6 December 2017).

23. Margaret Bolton, 'Loneliness – the state we're in', Age UK (2012). Available at https://www.campaigntoendloneliness.org/wp-content/uploads/Loneliness-The-State-Were-In.pdf (last visited 6 December 2017).

24. Steve Morris, 'Loneliness in older people is a scandal. Here's what one church is doing about it' 4 September 2017. Available at https://www.christiantoday.com/article/loneliness-in-older-people-is-a-scandal-heres-what-one-church-is-doing-about-it/113000.htm (last visited 6 December 2017).

25. The Gift of Years. Available at: https://www.brf.org.uk/thegiftofyears (last visited 29 November 2017).

26. Pilgrims' Friend Society. Available at: http://pilgrims.wpengine.com (last visited 29 November 2017).

Chapter 3: Tame It!

27. Benjamin Zander, 'The Transformative Power of Classical Music', TED. Available at: https://www.ted.com/talks/benjamin_zander_on_music_and_passion/transcript?language=en (last visited 29 November 2017).

28. 'Apollo 11: The computers that put man on the moon' ComputerWeekly. com. Available at: http://www.computerweekly.com/feature/Apollo-11-The-computers-that-put-man-on-the-moon (last visited 29 November 2017).

29. Robert B. Durham, *Modern Folklore* (published by Lulu.com, 2015), p.277.

30. Biography of Rosa Parks. Available at: https://www.biography.com/people/rosa-parks-9433715 (last visited 30 November 2017).

31. Susan Cain, *Quiet: The Power of Introverts in a World That Can't Stop Talking* (Penguin Books Limited, 2013), p.2.

32. 'EXCLUSIVE: James Blunt returns with his final Metro agony uncle column', 12 November 2014. Available at: http://metro.co.uk/2014/11/12/exclusive-james-blunt-returns-with-his-final-metro-agony-uncle-column-4945720/ (last visited 30 November 2017).

33. 'The Big Read', BBC, 2 September 2014. Available at: http://www.bbc.co.uk/arts/bigread/top100.shtml (last visited 30 November 2017).

34. 'Plunkett, William George (1910–1975)', Australian Dictionary of Biography, 2002. Available at http://adb.anu.edu.au/biography/plunkett-william-george-11439 (last visited 8 December 2017).

35. Tom Wright, *Bible Study Guides: James* (SPCK Publishing, 2012), p.39.

36. For example, Martin Luther (translated by Charles M. Jacobs and E. Theodore Bachmann), *Prefaces to the New Testament* (Wildside Press 2010), p.10.

Chapter 4: Lose It

37. David Field, *Discovering James* (Crossway Bible Guides, 1998), p.140.

38. Alec Motyer, *The Message of James,* Bible Speaks Today (IVP, 1985), p.141.

39. Explored by David Kinnaman, President of the Barna Group, *You Lost Me: Why Young Christians are Leaving the Church...And Rethinking Faith* (Baker Books, 2012).

40. C. S. Lewis, *Mere Christianity* (William Collins, UK edition, 2016).

41. Websites last visited 8 December 2017.

Chapter 5: Finish It

42. *Hupomeno* is specifically used in James 1:12 and James 5:11.

43. *Makrothumia* is also used in James 5:8 and James 5:10.

44. Kit Eaton, "How One Second Could Cost Amazon $1.6 Billion In Sales", Fast Company, 15 March 2012. Available at https://www.fastcompany. com/1825005/how-one-second-could-cost-amazon-16-billion-sales (last visited 8 December 2017.

45. For more on this concept and idea see Lester L. Grabbe, *A History of the Jews and Judaism in the Second Temple Period* (vol. 1) (T & T Clark International, new edition 2006).

46. Dietrich Bonhoeffer, *The Cost of Discipleship* (Simon and Schuster, 2012) p.89.

NOTE SPACE

_____

_____

_____

_____

_____

_____

_____

_____

_____

_____

_____

_____

_____

_____

_____

_____

_____

_____

_____

_____

_____

_____

_____

Ships *of* Mercy

In Africa alone lack of access to surgery is a greater killer each year than HIV, typhoid and malaria put together. With 75% of the world's population living within 150km of a port city, Mercy Ships can reach people who live with little or no healthcare in some of the poorest parts of the world.

Celebrating 40 years of Mercy Ships, this is the story of how a Colorado farm boy built a navy, how a decrepit ocean liner became a hospital and how a boat-load of volunteers is literally changing the face of the world … one person at a time.

The story of Don Stephens and his vision for Mercy Ships is simply breathtaking. His encounter with Mother Teresa shook his life to the core and I would challenge anyone not to be equally affected by reading Don's story here. – Gavin Calver

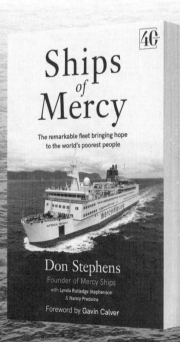

ISBN 978 1 473 68254 2